T. C. HAMMOND:
IRISH CHRISTIAN

T. C. HAMMOND: IRISH CHRISTIAN

His Life and Legacy in Ireland and Australia

✳

WARREN NELSON

THE BANNER OF TRUTH TRUST

THE BANNER OF TRUTH TRUST
3 Murrayfield Road, Edinburgh EH12 6EL
P.O. Box 621, Carlisle, Pennsylvania 17013, USA

*

© Warren Nelson 1994
First Published 1994
ISBN 0 85151 672 6

*

Typeset in 11½/13pt Adobe Garamond
Printed and bound in Great Britain by
BPC Paperbacks Ltd
A member of
The British Printing Company Ltd

With thanks for Harold 'Bluey' Dunstan
who challenged me with the logic of
'by grace you are saved'
and gave me a copy of
In Understanding Be Men

Contents

	Illustrations	ix
	Principal Dates	xi
	Foreword	xiii
	Preface	xv
1	Land of Saints and Sinners?	1
2	Evangelism in Victorian Ireland	10
3	The Boy Preacher	27
4	A Parish in Dublin	52
5	At The Irish Church Missions	65
6	'To Australia's Sunny Shore . . .'	92
7	Australia at Large	111
8	Books and Theology	131
9	Ireland After Hammond	145
	Appendices:	
I	The Writings of T. C. Hammond	159
II	The Wit and Wisdom of T. C. Hammond	167
III	Selected Bibliography	173
	Notes	175

Illustrations

Between pages 80 *and* 81

1. YMCA group in Cork (c.1895)
   Back row: centre, George Bird; extreme left, G.R.
   Harding Wood
   Centre row: centre, John McNay; on his right, T.C.
   Hammond

2. *top*: Hammond in ward of a children's home, Dublin
   bottom: Hammond, seated, centre right, with Mission
   workers in Dublin (c.1935)

3. The Inter-Varsity Fellowship Conference at Swanwick,
   Derbyshire, 1948. Hammond in bottom left corner,
   with Professor Rendle Short on his right. Many other
   contemporary and future evangelical leaders are also in
   this photograph, including Howard Mowll, Frank
   Houghton, Gwynne Walters, Verna Wright, Dick
   Lucas, Douglas Johnson and Leith Samuel

4. Hammond when Principal of Moore Theological
   College, Sydney

Principal Dates

20 February 1877	Birth
Spring, 1892	Conversion
20 December 1903	Ordained Deacon
1903	Curate, St Kevin's, Dublin
26 March 1905	Ordained Presbyter
January, 1906	Married
1910–1919	Rector, St Kevin's, Dublin
1919–1936	Superintendent Irish Church Missions
1926	Canadian/Australian visit
1936	Move to Australia
1936–1961	Rector, St Philip's, Sydney
1936–1953	Principal, Moore College
1939–1961	Cathedral Chapter, St Andrew's, Sydney
1943–1948	Bathurst Ritual Case
1949–1961	Archdeacon
1947–48	Visit to England & Ireland
16 November 1961	Death
11 January 1970	Death of Mrs Hammond

Foreword

Thomas Chatterton Hammond left an indelible mark on the church in two countries. Indeed as his students went out into many lands it is impossible to say where his influence ended. It is good that Warren Nelson has written a biography which will enable many in Ireland to see something of what he accomplished in Australia and many in Australia to recognise his greatness in the land of his birth.

There can be no doubt that the Anglican church in the diocese of Sydney owes much of its present position to the work T. C. Hammond accomplished. His work at Moore College gave that institution much of its present direction and established it as a bastion of evangelicalism and as a place of first-rate scholarship. And his contribution to the church's synods and councils was of the greatest importance. Indeed it can be said that he left his mark on the church throughout Australia through his contribution to the constitution by which its present life is ordered.

He was a very clear and logical thinker. He had a way of getting to the heart of any matter on which he was engaged and seeing exactly what was involved. He would sweep aside all the non-essentials and concentrate on what was relevant. In this book there is recorded his comment when someone said that he did not understand Karl Barth, 'Whose fault is that?' That says a lot about TC. He was rigorous in thinking any matter through until his own thought was clear and then in expressing the truth he saw in terms that anyone could understand. He had no patience with obscurity and took it as the duty of anyone who lectured or wrote that he should make himself clear. And he combined all this with an impish sense of humour. He did not take himself too seriously and found much to laugh about in life.

I have never forgotten his kindness to me when I was beginning my study of theology. I was teaching school at the time and trying to do the Th.L. diploma of the Australian College of Theology in my spare time. TC heard of me when I had done Part I, and invited me to see him as I started in on Part II. He discussed the course with me and then had me come every week through the academic year for a tutorial (shared by one other student) in doctrine. He treated the set syllabus and the necessity for passing the examination with lordly disdain but he fascinated me with the way he approached the general subject. He taught me to concentrate on the evidence rather than on scholarly opinion and he was merciless in exposing illogicality and bluster. To this day I am grateful for the insight he gave me into the way a scholar should go about his work.

T. C. Hammond was at home in the highest councils of the church and he made a great contribution there. But he was humble enough to give time and effort to helping unknown and insignificant students. That is a great combination.

LEON MORRIS

Preface

It is a remarkable thing that in the early and middle years of the twentieth century one of the smallest groups of evangelical believers in the English speaking world, that of the Irish Free State (after 1949 the Republic of Ireland), provided a considerable number of scholars and teachers who held significant positions in Theological and Bible Colleges. Alec Motyer was Principal of Trinity College, Bristol as was James O'Byrne earlier; H. D. McDonald was Vice-Principal of London Bible College; Hugh Jordan was Principal at London College of Divinity; Alan Cole was Master of Robert Menzies College, Macquarie University; H. L. Ellison was senior tutor at Moorlands Bible College. Peter Williams became Vice-Principal of Trinity, Bristol, and Victor Reid Principal of Redcliffe College. And from 1936 to 1953 another Irishman, the subject of this book, T. C. Hammond, was Principal of Moore Theological College, Sydney.

That such Christian leaders had to exercise their gifts outside their home country is part of the tragedy of Ireland. This book is written in the hope that the next generation of such scholars will not have to leave their homeland but will be able to teach in Ireland and bring biblical truth to bear on Irish life. It is also written to lay 'a small wreath on the grave of a great man'.[1]

These pages chronicle one small part of the story of the Irish Church. The word 'Church' is perhaps best left undefined for the moment. To some the Irish Church can only mean the largest denomination in Ireland, *i.e.* the Roman Catholic Church. For others the expression will mean the Church of Ireland, the Church which historically, but not in reality, can claim the *de jure* title of being the Irish Church, older than Canterbury, and much older than the first organised missions of the Roman Church to Ireland. Then there will be those for whom the expression will mean simply that part of the one true Church, the company of all believers, that resides in Ireland. T. C. Hammond had interaction with all three of these, and so the lack of definition is deliberate.

In his long life T. C. Hammond was called many things! From 'Tommy' in Victorian Cork, through 'Mr.' or 'Hammond', or 'Canon', 'Archdeacon', or 'TC', 'Princ' (*sic*), 'Uncle Tom', 'Old Tom', right on to the few who in his last years gave him his honorary 'Doctor'. Other than using the general 'Hammond' I have tried to reproduce the appropriate usage for time and place.

Throughout these pages I use the word 'evangelical' to describe those Christians who, accepting the Scriptures as God's infallible and authoritative word, stress man's fall and his redemption through the atoning substitutionary death of the Lord Jesus Christ, along with the necessity for the new birth and repentance and faith and who therefore endeavour to live godly lives. It has by no means the same meaning or connotations as the word 'Protestant'.

It would have been a pleasure to have been able to thank in print all those individuals who have helped me in so many different ways. These include those who gave me their recollections and their hospitality during my researches in Ireland and Australia; students of the Irish Bible School who did painstaking checking for me, some Australian friends and fellow teachers at the School who sieved out most, I hope, of my mistakes. The list of names, however, would exceed three hundred. Therefore with the exception of Hammond's son, Carl, his daughter, Doris, and Dr Leon Morris who has written the Foreword I must confine myself to thanking here the staff of those institutions which were helpful to me in different ways: Cork YMCA; Irish Church Missions, Dublin; Cork City Library; The Christian Brothers Community, Dun Laoghaire and Kells; The Representative Church Body Library, Dublin; Moore Theological College, Sydney; The Church Missionary Society, London; the Public Records Office, London. I am particularly grateful to Mrs Barbara King and Dawn Langrell for their painstaking typing.

This work is offered as a history of past events, not as a detailed pattern for the present or future. Hammond himself was cautious about the use of biographies, saying: 'To imitate details is to lose the wood for the trees and it may not be out of place to say that biographies, if we are to gather their full inspiration, should be used rather sparingly'. [2]

WARREN NELSON

Acknowledgements

The author is grateful to the following for permission to use extracts from material under their control:

Canon J. Crawford, St Patrick's Cathedral (St Kevin's Vestry Books).
The General Committee of the Irish Church Missions (various publications and record books).
Victor Tutty, Chairman, Cork YMCA (Minute Books of the Cork YMCA).
H. de Waard, Geelong, Victoria (extract from *Vox Reformata*).
Keith H. Percival, General Director of the Faith Mission (extract from *Bright Words*).

He is also grateful to the following publishers:
Marshall Pickering (extracts from T. C. Hammond, *Fading Light* and *Age-Long Questions*).
Inter-Varsity Press (extracts from T. C. Hammond, *Perfect Freedom*, *Reasoning Faith* and *In Understanding Be Men*).
Oxford University Press (extract from W. A. Phillips, ed., *History of the Church of Ireland, 1934*).
Dublin YMCA (extract from *A Century of Service*).

1

Land of Saints and Sinners?

Thomas Chatterton Hammond was a true Irishman; indeed he was a *Cork* man and proud of his distinctive origin. Sometimes he could not resist the temptation to comment that he was 'a man of weight' in order to see how long it took English or Australian people to realise he was joking. He loved Ireland and his fellow countrymen. In a speech delivered in London in 1922 (which excels even W. B. Yeats' famous 'no petty people' oration on Ireland and her people) he spoke with passion about his love for, and attachment to the land of his forebears:

I believe the root trouble of Ireland cannot be settled by an Act of Parliament. It is the heart of the people that wants changing, and until you remove the root cause of the trouble you cannot hope for peace and blessing in the land I love . . . for we are second to none, we Irish Protestants, in love to the country that gave us birth, and for the sky that hangs over us. Her valleys are ours, and her mountains. Her soil holds our sacred dead, and all the best treasures of that land have been won by our efforts. Therefore we love our country, and we make a fight for her still.[1]

But because he was also a Protestant many Irish people would not consider him to be authentically Irish. To understand why so simple and clear an equation has been made between being Irish and being Roman Catholic it is necessary to take a bird's eye view of several centuries of Irish history.

Ireland is a religious paradox. How could a small island which still has one of the highest rates of church attendance in the world be a home for religious war? Detractors of the Christian faith point to Ireland and say 'That is Christianity for you!' and often Christian apologists can only mumble excuses. In fact inter-community strife in Ireland is not simply a matter of religious beliefs, nor are the participants theologically motivated. But there is enough religious colouring in the Irish context to make the charges stick. The struggle for power in tribal politics does, for the most part, run in the river bed carved out by earlier religious controversies.

SAINT PATRICK

Christianity was planted in Ireland in the fifth century by Patrick. Scholars still disagree about his personal origins and whether he was from England, Wales, or perhaps even a Scot. Various legends have attached themselves to his name, notably the tradition that he used the shamrock to demonstrate the Trinity and that he banished snakes from the country. Both legends are without foundation.

Partisanship has often obscured the real Patrick by seeking to claim him as either a devout Roman Catholic or as a Protestant. In fact he was neither. But beyond doubt, as his extant writings make clear, he was well-read in the Scriptures and had a simple, but informed, faith in God which encompassed the incarnation, Christ's victory over sin and death, and the gift of the Holy Spirit to make us sons of God. He was completely silent on centralised church authority, and on such other accretions to biblical Christianity as purgatory and the doctrine of the sacrificial mass.

For Patrick, Ireland (then known by its Latin name *Hibernia*), was 'the last place on earth'. He had been taken there as a prisoner while a youth and spent six years in virtual slavery among heathen people before he managed to escape. But in response to a Macedonian call he returned. While he was by no means the first to bring Christianity to Ireland, through his ministry it was able to take root and grow.

The Christian faith flourished through Patrick's work and those who followed him gave Ireland the reputation of being the 'Land of Saints and Scholars'.

In the fifth century the Roman Empire was folding back on its own heartlands; hordes from the East were sweeping across Europe. Christianity was being extinguished. But in Ireland (where the Roman Empire never extended) the flame was kept alive. By the efforts of Irish monks and missionaries who 'wandered about for Christ' the fire was re-kindled in Britain and Europe.

The names of these men continue to reverberate with their deeds: Columba of Derry who founded Iona in northern Britain as another Antioch; Brendan who visited Iceland and possibly America; Columbanus who travelled in France, Switzerland and down to Italy, and one of whose companions gave his name to the present Swiss town of St Gallen.

This missionary activity came to its peak in the seventh century, but was cut short when Ireland in her turn received the rapacious attention of hordes similar to those that had earlier spilled across Europe. To Ireland they came as the seaborne Vikings from Scandinavia. But as the years passed, the raiders were in time christianised and communications between the continent and Ireland were opened again.

Sadly, the Christianity being introduced to Ireland then was very different from that which Patrick had earlier brought. The Irish were misled into submitting to Rome and the Irish Church lost both its independence and its vitality. Ever since, Irish Christianity has tended to be subservient to the theologies of other places. The Irish have taken, second-hand, the teaching and the controversies of Rome, Canterbury, Edinburgh or America, along with the lesser emphases of religious movements outside their shores.

The coming of a more developed Catholicism brought changes. Irish Christianity had followed the family and clan structure of society; it was monastic and under the leadership of abbots. Now foreign bishops ruled. The newly imported form of Christianity brought a different date for Easter and the Roman style of tonsure. The simpler, genuine faith was overlaid with superstitions and fables growing eventually to full medievalism. Significantly, students no longer travelled to Ireland to study the Scriptures.

In 1110 the country was divided into dioceses and in 1152, seven hundred years after Patrick, four Archbishops, (Armagh, Cashel, Tuam, and Dublin) were given the pallium to wear, signifying submission to the See of Rome. At about the same time (through a different series of events) the English came and began to impose their rule under the Norman king, Henry II.

It is at this point that we meet one of the paradoxes of Irish Christianity: it was *England* that brought Ireland under the authority of Rome and subsequently the Catholic Church imposed Englishmen as Bishops and leaders on the Irish Church. Indeed by one of the Statutes of Kilkenny (1367) it became illegal for Irishmen to hold office in the Church in those areas under English jurisdiction. The partnership of Roman Catholicism and nationalism is, therefore, not intrinsic or fundamental to the Irish culture:

Here Patriotism and Romanism have become almost interchangeable terms. A strange misalliance, no doubt—when it is remembered that it was a Pope who first robbed Ireland of her independence, and that it was an English invader who was the first to establish in Ireland the supremacy of Rome. Be it so. And those who attack the strongholds of Rome must expect, for a time at least, to be regarded as attacking Irish nationality as well. This in itself is a terrible difficulty.[2]

THE REFORMATION FAILURE

When the Reformation came to Europe in the sixteenth century and the dust of ages was blown off biblical truths, Ireland's history and geography left her at a disadvantage. Little or none of the Renaissance revival of learning had reached her shores nor were the Scriptures available in the language of the people. Consequently the liberating truths which elsewhere brought radical spiritual change—justification by faith, the priesthood of all believers and the private appeal to Scripture—did not reach the Irish people at large. As a result, there remained only the enforced political aspects of the Reformation by which few Irish people were impressed or moved.

England tried to impose the Reformation through statute by a combination of 'stick and carrot', starting in 1539 but without serious effort until the 1590s. Even then English law had little effect outside the eastern coastal counties known as the Pale. Little was done to carry Reformation truth to people's hearts. Some of the Irish bishops, such as Browne of Dublin, were keen on reform, but others put a very low value on truth. Notorious among the latter was Miler McGrath of Cashel who had been in turn a Franciscan friar, the Roman Catholic bishop of Down and the Protestant Archbishop of Cashel. His loyalty to any cause was always up for auction.

Only in the reign of Elizabeth I were efforts made to translate the Prayer Book and Bible into Irish. Later Bishop Bedell also set about translating the Bible and training his clergy to preach in Irish. Then, in the early part of the seventeenth century, James Ussher applied his great learning to the problem and produced an Irish theological credal standard, *The Irish Articles* (1615). But it was too late. The people had made up their minds; the Reformation had come in English clothes and they wanted no part of it.

Thus the spirit of nationalism, the very force which had helped the progress of the Reformation in Germany and England, acted against it in Ireland. The lines were drawn and subsequent centuries did nothing to change them. All that happened in the passing years was that they were dug deeper.

Various land settlements, euphemistically described as 'plantations' but in fact 'confiscations', cemented the status quo by bringing land ownership into the equation. Risings and rebellions were put down and stiffer and stiffer laws imposed. Consequently, battles fought 300 years ago are still remembered as vividly as those of World War II.

The intervening years did not contribute to a healing of the memories. Protestants rested in their political ascendancy, Roman Catholics, bewailing their confiscations and their past, drew closer and closer to their Church. The English had unwittingly made a stick to beat themselves with, as Archbishop Plunkett wrote:

England has made an unrestful bed for herself, and she must lie upon it. If she is scourged, she furnished the rod herself. In the twelfth century Romish England planted Popery in Ireland. The upas tree was an exotic unknown in the country; the soil was prepared by treachery; and the instrument of the actual transplanting was the sword. Upon the coincidence, solitary in all history, when an English pope could conspire with an English king, this baneful act was accomplished, and so Ireland became popish. When, in the sixteenth century, the dark cloud of Romanism was rolled off the shores of England, by that 'wind' that 'bloweth where it listeth', no prayerful pains were taken to carry on its course over the sister island; to 'say to the wind, Come from the four winds, O breath, and breathe upon these slain, that they may live'. Laws were made to anglicise the Irish, instead of efforts to Christianise them. The royal supremacy of the King of England was established, and not the supremacy of the Majesty on high. The means employed consisted of Acts of Parliament, and not the Book of God.[3]

On both sides there was an identification of church and politics. Church membership became as much a matter of patriotism as of faith and a means of 'not letting the side down'. The post-Reformation centuries came and went, but there was little spiritual vision in either Roman Catholic or Protestant community. Church leaders from both sides settled into their place in society. It was assumed that Ireland was a Christian country needing only a little morality and a check on some of the worst excesses.

By the end of the eighteenth century Irish Catholicism

was slowly coming out from under the worst of the Penal Laws although it was still common for Roman Catholic worship to be conducted in rough shelters by priests in lay clothes. Meanwhile, Protestantism in its Anglican form was virtually an acquiescent arm of Government. Presbyterianism, largely brought in with the plantations, was more radical and at that time closer to the aspirations of nationalism. In College Green, Dublin, an Irish Parliament, though only representative of the Protestant Ascendancy, concerned itself with Irish industries and made noises about nationhood.

THE ACT OF UNION

1800 is not only an easy date to remember, but one which serves as an authentic new genesis point in Irish history. The short-lived independence of the Irish Parliament did not give the stability and security needed in the face of threats from revolutionary France. The rebellion of 1798, for the most part confined to the Roman Catholics of the South East, some radical Presbyterians of the North East, and a French landing in Mayo, had caused fright to many in authority. From London it seemed that only a complete Union would meet the threats of the hour and give a basis for a better relationship between England and Ireland.

In 1800, after well-documented persuasion and bribery, the Irish parliamentarians voted themselves out of authority in Dublin, and settled for a reduced number of seats in London. The Roman Catholic bishops were in favour of the Union, as the best means of achieving greater freedom and full emancipation. The majority of Church of Ireland bishops voted for it, but for different reasons. For them it promised the security of being part of a larger entity with an overwhelming Protestant majority. The Church of Ireland for a time relinquished her independence and became part of 'The United Church of England and Ireland', and the Union Jack gained the red saltire cross of St. Patrick.

The Napoleonic Wars cemented this Union with a closing of ranks in the face of a common danger. They also brought some prosperity to land owners and provided a social safety valve through the recruitment of young men for military service. The coast of Ireland was fortified with Martello towers. Apart from the idealistic gesture of rebellion by Robert Emmet in 1803, Ireland was quiet—at least for a while.

2

Evangelism in Victorian Ireland

B y the Nineteenth century deep-seated religious
change was underway in Ireland. Inevitably it took
longer to manifest itself than the political changes
had done. But like a slow fire it burned quietly and
inwardly at first before giving warmth and light to many. In
the Church of Ireland the dull and deadening Deism of
the previous century was giving place to an evangelical
awakening. The influence of Methodism was spreading.

John Wesley paid no less than twenty-one visits to
Ireland. He had a great love for the country and left
behind many followers scattered throughout the land and
well-organised in classes and societies. One of his foremost
early lieutenants was the Irishman Thomas Walsh. George
Whitefield also visited briefly, having been all but ship-
wrecked near Limerick. From there he had travelled
overland to Dublin preaching occasionally. People of influence also travelled to and from England for health, family
or business reasons and brought back with them the books
and sermons of the Evangelical Awakening. Between
England and Ireland there was a free interchange of clergymen, and many senior clergy in Ireland were English in any
case. Soldiers on military duty also became seed carriers.

Thus, before the Union was twenty-five years old a movement, profound enough to be called 'The Second Reformation' by friend and foe alike, was well underway.

A fresh vitality thus entered Irish Christianity. God was no longer seen as the Deist's remote First Cause who, having made and wound up the world, had left it to its own devices. He was no longer merely the interesting, but harmless, conclusion of a clever philosophical proof nor the Ultimate Moralist and Object of Duty. In church and meeting place, in cottage and 'Big House', God was once again recognized as the loving Father who had sent his Son to live and teach, and to give himself on the cross to reconcile us to God. Rationalistic books were put away, the Bible was brought out; ribaldry died down to be replaced by hymn singing; the hunting, shooting and fishing parson and the absentee bishop (or sometimes worse, since there had been some episcopal scandals) gave place to men concerned with biblical truth and evangelism.

Three very different figures illustrate the reality of this change:

Robert Daly, a son of Irish gentry, was one. Being shown on a map the area of the mission work on Achill Island he admitted that he knew that countryside well from the days when he thought: 'God had sent him into the world for no higher purpose than to slaughter grouse.'[1] But he was challenged by the gospel and converted. He later became an evangelical bishop (Cashel 1843-72).

Gideon Ouseley (1762-1839) of Dunmore, County Galway, traversed Ireland as an itinerant Methodist missionary, often preaching in Irish. In earlier days he had lived for drink and gambling and bore the scars of brawls. Then the strange behaviour of a detachment of Dragoon Guards arrested his conscience and brought him to a new spiritual seriousness. On coming to town, the soldiers had taken a public room in the inn and were singing hymns! When his father later complained of his preaching forays Gideon pointed out that when he had spent whole nights in sin no one had expressed the least concern!

A third figure, Hyacinth D'Arcy, was the aristocratic landlord and proprietor of the town and region around Clifden in West Galway, until changed fortunes and Christian convictions led him to become a clergyman serving in his very own town, living in a small street house, the butt of abuse and ridicule.

THE WORK OF THE SECOND REFORMATION

No one who has found Christ as 'the pearl of great price' will be surprised to read that such men wanted others to have what they had found. Their first sphere of evangelism was their own immediate circle and their fellow churchmen. Here they met both encouragement and resistance. Senior clergy were alarmed. As a result, students of Trinity College were forbidden to attend Bethesda Church in Dorset Street, Dublin (a privately built church and renowned evangelical preaching place, opened in 1784).

In Kilkenny, the Rev Peter Roe wanted to form a clerical society for Bible study. He was blocked, although, as he pointed out, eight local clergy could belong to the Hunt Club.

When such evangelical ministers were accused of going against the bishops, they challenged their overseers to give the lead in preaching and spreading the gospel. Then they would gladly follow. When they were described as 'not true churchmen' they rightly defended themselves as ministers who were faithful to the Thirty-Nine Articles.

It was not long before these men developed a deep concern for the spiritual needs of their Roman Catholic countrymen. How could they withhold such good news from the overwhelming majority of their neighbours?

All subsequent evangelistic efforts, frequently criticised as they were, have to be seen in the light of this simple loving concern. Unwise things were done, no doubt, and later the cause of evangelism became sadly entwined with the politics of the Protestant Ascendancy. But the original motivating force was as old as the love which drove Andrew to tell his brother about Jesus. All the committees for evangelism, the schools, the evangelistic missions and selling of Bibles sprang from that. When these faithful Christians were accused of proselytising they replied that if that meant discharging their sacred duty to proclaim the truth as they understood it, then they were indeed guilty.

As the nineteenth century advanced so did the work. The earnest and well reasoned preaching of the Rev M. R. Mathias at Bethesda, in Dublin, influenced many leading city churchmen. It became a recognised gathering point for country visitors. One such was John Gregg (1798-1878) from Clare who grew up knowing little of God but became an outstanding preacher, direct and forceful. He was an Irish J. C. Ryle. Trinity Church in Lower Gardiner Street, Dublin was built around his ministry (closed as a church building in 1914, it became the busiest unemployment office in Dublin). Gregg later became Bishop of Cork, and during his time St Finnbarre's Cathedral was built.

The spiritual awakening also affected the outlying countryside, despite the bitter legacy of the Tithe Wars of the 1830s when the resistance of Roman Catholics to paying a tax for clergy they did not want came to a head. In Doon and Pallas Green on the Tipperary-Limerick border there was a remarkable spiritual awakening. When Bishop Daly of Cashel visited for Confirmation services he found hundreds of converts. Nor were these 'converts' merely in the sense of denominational proselytes, but new men and women in Christ. A visiting clergyman who was conscientious in examining whether they were truly aware of what they were doing and properly informed in their faith concluded after questioning them:

They never failed in producing scriptural proof for any of the truths on which I examined them, and were always prepared with the chapter and verse to which they had occasion to refer. There was also such an appearance of heart and earnest faith amongst them, more especially when I spoke of the great doctrines of salvation, such as justification by faith and a free pardon through the blood of the Lamb, that I can only say, that if they were not sincere converts, they were the most awful and successful hypocrites with whom it has ever been my misfortune to come in contact. I only wish that some of our cold lukewarm Protestant professors could have witnessed the zeal and apparent joy with which these poor converts proved, from the word of God, that the only justification of the gospel is through the free grace of their crucified and risen Lord.[2]

The Bishop himself described it as a most glorious day in every sense of the word.

There were amazing advances in remote western areas. Edward Nangle, born in Athboy, County Meath, in 1799, was invited to travel on a ship bringing relief to Achill

Island, County Mayo in 1831. He was appalled at the condition of the people and at the spiritual darkness. In some ways they were little removed from paganism and were without the ministry of either Roman Catholic or Protestant clergy. With the support of the Archbishop of Tuam, Nangle began a work that led to a colony being built and large numbers coming to faith in Christ. At Ventry on the Dingle Peninsula, County Kerry there were similar conversions and three local landlords became prominent in preaching the gospel.

THE IRISH CHURCH MISSIONS
The work of the Irish Church Missions (with which T. C. Hammond was later to be intimately connected) had its origins about the same time. Alexander Dallas, an Englishman who had been at the Battle of Waterloo as a young officer, was converted to Christ by unusual means. Once, while riding in the dark only the instinct of his horse saved him from going over a cliff. He was made to think of the issue of death then, and later to consider the mystery of life when his first child was born. After some time he began to work for a mission to Jews, for whom he had a special affection. In the providence of God, this brought him to Ireland where he saw the terrible need and darkness of the Irish.

Dallas had developed considerable organisational skills in the Army, and now had the idea of using the postal system (which was something of a novelty in itself), for evangelism. He arranged for 23,000 letters, each containing an assortment of evangelistic literature, to be posted in order to arrive simultaneously at homes all over Ireland on the 16th of January 1846. From that event the Mission grew until at the end of the nineteenth century it had travelling evangelists and Scripture readers in every part of Ireland.

In the meantime, Methodists were increasingly establishing themselves as a separate denomination. This was, no doubt, partly because they had their share of the divisiveness that has often blighted the church, but also because of opposition in the Established Church. Non-evangelicals objected to their gospel preaching, while friction between their Arminianism and the basic Calvinism within the Church was increasing. A further reason had to do with tactics. Methodists wanted some form of ordination because their preachers and evangelists considered themselves at a disadvantage in debate with Roman Catholic priests, since they seemed to lack any ecclesiastical 'standing'. Throughout Ireland they had considerable success, mostly in pockets of the country where their legacy still remains.

Presbyterians, who were very much stronger in the North, were not as deeply involved in evangelism in the South, partly because they were only slowly emerging from an almost fatal battle with unitarianism within their own membership. However when they did send faithful missionaries, sharing the same message and methods, they too reaped a spiritual harvest. The much smaller Baptist denomination was also actively engaged in the same work to an extent out of all proportion to its numbers.

Others were awakened where no evangelists worked. There was the extraordinary case of Thomas Connellan, who was ordained as a Roman Catholic priest in 1882. His own study of the Bible led him seriously to doubt his Church's doctrine of transubstantiation (the teaching that in the mass the bread and wine become the body and blood of Christ). This became such a crisis of mind for him that he made a dramatic departure by pretending he had drowned in the Shannon near Athlone, where he worked on the staff of the Cathedral. He travelled to London, and found his way to St Paul's Church, Onslow Square, where the Rev M. R. Webb-Pebloe had the joy of leading him into the full light of the gospel. Meanwhile Connellan's boat and priest's clothes had been found along the banks of the river. The townspeople were convinced that he had drowned. The newspapers were filled with warm tributes to his Catholic piety and other virtues.

Some time later, Connellan became convinced that he should return to Ireland to declare his faith and his reasons for leaving the Church of Rome. He was attacked by a crowd in Athlone and later excommunicated by the Church. However when his character was vilified, his friends only needed to produce the glowing newspaper accounts of his life as a priest to silence the critics! In 1890 he was licensed (not re-ordained) as a clergyman by the Church of Ireland. He set up the Connellan Mission, and began a monthly evangelical paper called *The Catholic* which he edited until his death. His successor as editor was T. C. Hammond.

THE SCRIPTURES

The priority of all the evangelical agencies was to get the Bible or portions of it into people's hands, knowing that much depended on the reading of God's word in line with the assertion that 'the entrance of thy word brings light' (*Psa.* 119:130). Evangelicals had personally experienced this illumination and liberation, and believed that if people could read the Bible for themselves they too would be blessed.

In this great work, evangelicals had to overcome various difficulties. Many people could not read, so schools were established. Lay Scripture readers were sent out. Of those who could read many read only Irish. As a counter-measure work was done to train readers in Irish, leading to the starting of the 'Irish Society' in 1818, which later amalgamated with the Irish Church Missions.

Roman Catholics were hostile to 'Protestant' Bibles. This often was a camouflage for resistance to any Bible. To reduce prejudice whenever possible, Scripture readers and itinerant Bible sellers ('colporteurs'), used the Douay Version (translated from Latin at Rheims and Douai in Flanders from 1610).

Most Douay versions had notes which represented traditional Roman Catholic theology, but the societies were able to get hold of an edition published with the *imprimatur* of the Roman Catholic bishops but which had been printed without notes (the 'Coyne' edition). This became the standard tool of evangelism and continued in use until the 1960s. Some evangelicals objected that there were serious mistranslations in the Douay, such as 'do penance' for 'repent', (*Matt*. 3:2; 4:17, *Luke* 13:3, 5). But the more pragmatic reasoned that it was better for people to have a flawed copy of Scripture than none at all.

No matter what version was used the opposition to the spread of the Scriptures was fierce. Irishmen to-day who can pick and choose among versions and can buy a Bible even in a small provincial town should remember that it is not so long since the Bible was, in effect, forbidden; Bibles were burned and those who sold them were whipped out of Irish towns.

To this period also belongs what was called 'The Roman

Controversy'. The word 'controversy' is here used in its older sense of a debate or disputation, not in its more usual modern sense of being quarrelsome or discordant. It was commonplace for public debates to be organised between Roman Catholic and Protestant speakers, and these were widely advertised, reported in the papers, and usually conducted amicably. One debate in 1827 extended over six days. But the proceedings were often bogged down in quotations and counter-quotations from the Fathers of the early Church—a rich source of red herrings. In this connection Archbishop Whately had once asked people quoting the Fathers to state 'which ones they meant' and 'whether they themselves had read them'!

SPREAD AND DECLINE

The 'Second Reformation' was not only represented by courageous evangelists travelling round the country—often where there were no roads—to bring good news to simple peasants in smoky cabins. The middle and upper classes were also affected; for example, C. S. Parnell, leader of the landless (although himself a landlord), had a near relative known as 'Tract Parnell'. The movement which later became known as the Plymouth Brethren, was a child of evangelicals mostly from the Church of Ireland. John Nelson Darby, one of its most prominent leaders, had held a curacy in County Wicklow.

Lady Powerscourt, also from County Wicklow (an Irish Samuel Rutherford as a Christian letter writer and an Irish Countess of Huntingdon in her concern about the welfare of the church), had a circle of upper-class friends attending Bible studies at her home. Sadly her interests became more and more refined and speculative. She came under some influence from the Scot Edward Irving, sometimes regarded as a forerunner of the charismatic movement, and some evangelicals felt bound to break with her.

In the 1860s there were at least six bishops of the Church of Ireland who were unashamedly evangelical: O'Brien of Ossory Diocese, author of a classic work on justification by faith and a doughty opponent of rising Anglo-Catholicism; Daly of Cashel and Gregg of Cork, both already mentioned; Singer of Meath; Verschole of Kilmore, who wrote on the Psalms; and Plunkett of Tuam, who aided and defended the evangelistic efforts in the West.

It was thus a well-led and largely united Church that faced and survived the crisis of Disestablishment in 1869, which was seen by many as the first step in dismantling the Union. It was a step for which Gladstone was assured of the prayers of Spurgeon among nonconformists on one side and a Roman Catholic bishop on the other! Disestablishment was right, but its cause was advanced for the wrong reasons. Being a part of the Establishment, especially in Ireland, helped the Church only in some inconsequential externals while it harmed it spiritually. Gladstone acted only from political expediency.

Despite the remarkable achievements of evangelicals, the so-called 'Second Reformation' touched only a small proportion of Irish people. Sadly the simple preaching of the good news of forgiveness and new life in Christ was misrepresented and rejected; superstitious ceremonies continued to engulf the people in ignorance and a fear which was devoid of joy and peace with God.

Why was it that in England the Evangelical Awakening transformed society, while in Ireland it only scratched the surface? Apart from spiritual reasons, which lie in the hand of God, there were several practical reasons. It was never a movement of the majority of the population who, being Roman Catholics, rejected it as 'foreign'. Here lies a further irony of Irish religious life. At this time the more Italian party was gaining ascendancy in the Roman Catholic Church, and continental cults such as devotion to the Sacred Heart of Jesus were being introduced. In addition, the Protestant Church was submerged by a growing awareness of nationalism, but unfortunately its leaders did little to identify themselves with the interests and culture of the Irish people.

In stark contrast with the Protestant leadership were such men as the Roman Catholic Archbishops, Croke of Cashel and McHale of Tuam, who outrightly associated themselves with everything Irish. Also, as could be expected, the Church of Rome did not sit back and allow evangelicals to make inroads unchallenged. From the 1850s onwards there were constant 'Missions' to call back the wavering, usually taken by religious orders such as the Redemptorists.

Towards the end of the century other factors distracted the evangelicals in the Church of Ireland where a very small party of ritualists, influenced by developments in England, were re-introducing various ceremonies as a cover for doctrines that were a denial of the first Reformation, hence also of the second. Much more seriously, the rising tide of modernism began to damage the Church and influence some of her leading teachers. The so-called 'assured results' of Higher Criticism (often later to be revised and even discredited) shook people's confidence in God's word. Some pulpits became places to examine doubts rather than to proclaim saving truths.

THE FAMINE AND 'SOUPERISM'
The disaster of the Great Famine of 1845-1847, with other local famines before and after, reduced the Irish population between 1847 and 1861 by two million through death and emigration. It also set back the course of reformation. Some of the areas in the west and south-west which had experienced church growth were worst affected. Some of the converts died, while hundreds more emigrated taking their faith with them to more hospitable shores. In addition, the famines naturally engendered such a hatred of perceived culprits as to make evangelism exceptionally difficult in the second half of the century.

Part of this hatred attached itself to subsequent mission work by describing it as 'Souperism', a highly emotive term that retains potency even to-day in Ireland.[3] It comes from the accusation that Protestants used famine relief (which often came in the form of great boilers of soup), to woo Roman Catholics into a change of religion. It produced its own folklore and songs:

> Don't sell your souls,
>   for penny rolls and cheeks of hairy bacon

and

> Souper, souper on the wall
>   half a loaf would feed ye all,
> A farthing candle will give ye light
>   to read the Bible on Friday night.[4]

These accusations have been so widely accepted as proven that they deserve some consideration. It is possible that a small minority of Protestants offered relief for the wrong reasons, just as a few Roman Catholics may have professed conversion for the wrong reasons. But for the majority, especially for those who were engaged in evangelism, the charge was false. For them the Famine was a disaster and a heartbreaking reversal.

It is a matter of record that the work of evangelism and Bible distribution was going on long before the Famine. The Famine brought terrible loss to Christian workers too. Some of them beggared themselves for the people; others died from fever contracted in the course of their ministrations. These included Dr Traill of Schull, West Cork and the Hardcastles, the Baptist pastor in Waterford and his wife. Vital Christians caught up in such a tragedy would naturally do what they could to give relief to the crying need. Furthermore, the theology of the evangelicals denied the very idea that a little soup could bring about the 'new creation' they looked for in every convert. That could be accomplished only by a sovereign work of God.

THE '59 REVIVAL

An analysis of the 1859 Revival is not properly a part of this story. Its beginnings lay outside Ireland, although before it came there was a growing spirit of expectancy, and large meetings for prayer were being held.[5] It brought great blessing to the North of Ireland, some of which overflowed southward into Protestant churches. It arrested many.

In various ways the effects of those days continue into the present. Elsie Sandes and Dr Barnardo, founders of Soldiers' and Children's Homes respectively, were two Irish people affected by it who later would become well-known. Like all revivals, it too had its excesses in heated meetings, strong emotional surges, claims to see the devil, and newly converted people being plunged out of their depths into secondary issues. But the overall relationship to the indigenous work of the Second Reformation was weak.

Meanwhile a change was coming over the Roman Catholic Church in Ireland. It had entered the century poor and somewhat servile. Priests dressed in civilian clothes, less than half the people attended mass, of whom many were satisfied just to hear the consecration bell. Many services, including weddings, were held in the homes of the people because there were not enough church buildings, or because those available were considered inadequate. The Roman Catholic Church was still suffering from the effects of the Reformation, land confiscation and the Penal Laws. It was certainly not the church of recent twentieth century memory. Slowly, however, confidence was returning to the Roman Church. Many provisions of the Penal Laws had never been enforced and most had been removed by 1793. Nationalism, so detrimental to evangelicalism, served the Catholic Church well since at all levels the clergy identified themselves with the people in their sufferings and aspirations as well as in their dark grudges against landlords and the English. The Napoleonic wars made it almost impossible for priests to train on the continent and the College in Maynooth, County Kildare, founded in 1795, began to take a greater part in training priests. Students on the continent had had Gallican teachers (*i.e.* French, and therefore liberal and somewhat independent of Rome), but increasingly the Catholic Church in Ireland took an Ultramontane position (meaning 'beyond the mountains', *i.e.* with an Italian orientation and subservient to the Vatican).

For a considerable period (from 1850 until 1878) Archbishop, later Cardinal, Cullen had great influence, to the extent that the word 'Cullenization' was coined. He had no love for Protestants, and boasted that he had never eaten with one in his life. He also tried to revive an old regulation preventing his priests from doing so. He was determined to put the stamp of Rome on the Irish Church.

The result of these factors was an assertive, confident, political and conservative Roman Catholicism. Church building went on all over the country. The results of this expansion can still be seen in almost every town in Ireland: the Roman Catholic church is often a prominent ornate mid-nineteenth century building, contrasting with the Church of Ireland building which is usually much older, and often in the original part or centre of the town.

At home the Catholic Church was engaged in a vast work of religious and political consolidation, pushing nearer and nearer to making 'Irish' and 'Catholic' synonymous. Abroad the Roman faith followed the Irish emigrants and the British Empire contained a mirror image in a spiritual Irish empire. By the 1930s one third of the Roman Catholic bishops in the world had Irish surnames.

The clash of theologies, the protecting of converts at all costs (thus minimising their opportunities to witness to their families and former friends), and the apparent narrowness of evangelicals must be understood against the background of this strident nineteenth century Irish Catholicism. Late twentieth century models from other countries or even from Ireland itself are inappropriate measuring rods.

It is very easy to underestimate the opposition Irish evangelicals had to resist. Insidious pressures were brought to bear in homes and work places as well as in more obvious forms in civic life. English evangelicals may have thought their Irish counterparts stubborn or simply 'Irish', but they did not know what it was to grapple with Roman Catholicism when it held power. Despite valiant efforts the gospel and its effects had made little headway. At the end of the nineteenth century there was little that was different in the overall Irish religious scene.

3

The Boy Preacher

Tommy Hammond, the child of his father's old age, was born almost at the mid-point of Queen Victoria's reign. This made him a contemporary of Sean O'Casey the playwright, W. P. Nicholson the evangelist, and a little older than Eamon De Valera, later Prime Minister and President of Ireland. In terms of world figures he was of Churchill's generation.

The youngest child of Colman Mark Hammond and his second wife Elizabeth (*née* Sarjeant), Tommy was born on 20 February 1877 in Ashburton Villas, Cork.

The Hammonds were an old Cork family. His grandfather had been a ship's broker in Queenstown (Cobh), and, according to a 1794 licence, they had owned, in times past, the rights to be 'Gaugers and searchers for taking account of all Beers, Ales, Wort, Washes, Low Wines, Singlings, Spirits, Strong Waters, Brandy, Aqua Vitae, and all other liquors'.[1]

Cork was an old city claiming to go back eight centuries to Saint Finnbarr. But even here the Victorian order of things was firmly in place and running as smoothly as its own engineering achievements. Years later, when in his seventies and addressing a convention in Adelaide, Hammond showed his regard for the world order of his youth when he commented in an aside on 'The Great Victorian Age—and make no mistake, it was great, notwithstanding the stupid strictures sometimes passed upon it'.[2] Indeed he claimed that during a Royal visit in his childhood he slipped through a cordon and ran to Queen Victoria who waved back those trying to catch him and patted him on the head.[3]

The Empire was close to its zenith. The 'rich man' was 'in his castle'. More precisely, in Cork, he was being buried from it, for the week Tommy Hammond was born the local papers were full of the magnificent obsequies of the Earl of Bandon with full lists of mourners given in proper pecking order, and a description of his coronet being carried on a crimson velvet cushion in the state coach by his steward. The middle class was prospering and upwardly mobile; the traders, bankers, wine importers and small manufacturers of the city were enjoying the fruits of *Pax Britannica* and economic growth.

But 'the poor man' was also 'at his gate', sometimes sparing the soles of his boots by hanging them about his neck as he walked on smoother ground. The division between rich and poor was made all the deeper in Ireland by nationalism and religion since, with few exceptions, the wealthy were also Protestants and usually pro-British. The Hammond family, however, despite being Protestants, were finding it hard to maintain standards. Colman Hammond had been a missionary for a short time in Sierra Leone in the early 1850s with the Church Missionary Society (CMS). Sierra Leone was of importance then for the anti-slavery movement and British ships landed freed slaves there. But it was also a disease-ridden place and had earned the sobriquet 'the white man's grave'. Colman lost his first wife there, a victim of fever. Subsequently he had a good, if undistinguished, career as a Master in the Royal Navy, and had been at the Crimea. However he was involved in the grounding of his ship, HMS *Virago*, on the rocks of St George's Bay, Bermuda in 1861 in atrocious weather. This mishap was compounded on the voyage back to England when a navigational mix-up almost brought them onto rocks on the French coast. This disaster was averted only when Captain Hammond recognized the type of shingle they brought up as they took soundings.

The Admiralty took disciplinary proceedings and brought him before a court martial. His defence in his own hand is extant. A sincere and competent officer fell victim to the failures of crew members for whom he bore ultimate responsibility. The Admiralty acted on the letter of the law and Colman Hammond was forced to take early retirement.

After leaving the Navy, Captain Hammond lived for a while in the city before moving to a farm about ten miles out of Cork near Queenstown (now Cobh). Here young Tommy saw rural life close up. He later spoke of being taught the lore of the country and where the nest of the 'thrush, wren and lark' were. He also recalled the bonfires on the hills to celebrate the release of Michael Davitt from jail. Davitt (1846-1906) was a leading figure in the Irish Republican Brotherhood who was imprisoned several times for firearms dealing and sedition. Founder of the Irish Land League he was also elected as a Member of Parliament on several occasions. Hammond was only five at the time and called it 'my first introduction to the stormy scenes of Irish political life'.[4]

Tommy also remembered a humorous incident which struck him as characteristic of Cork. Once C. S. Parnell the Protestant politician and leader of the Irish Nationalist group, which forced the Home Rule Bill for Ireland on the Liberal Party under Gladstone, was visiting the city after the split in his party. Feelings were running high, and supporters were shouting 'Three cheers for Parnell' when a cabman of the other faction added 'and for Kitty O'Shea' (who was divorced from her husband in 1890 on the grounds of adultery with Parnell—whom she later married).

In 1883, when Hammond was only six, his father died. As the only son at home, though still a child, Tommy was sent off alone in a carriage to the funeral. It was still not the custom for women to attend. Despite his tender age at the time, he remembered the funeral music and the fact that he was later joined in the carriage by two officers with plumed hats and swords.

The farm was sold, and the pleasant country home had to be exchanged for a succession of modest houses in the city.

THE CORK YMCA

In that era Cork was no small cog in the British Empire. Good newspapers, efficient railways, the telegraph system and, most of all, the traffic of ships in its safe and commodious harbour kept a world outlook before people's attention. The Cork Exhibition of 1883 had attracted the best in craftsmanship from Europe and America. With trade and commerce also came the politicians, musicians and speakers of that optimistic world.

Such visitors were well received and provided for, unlike those other transients of the Empire, common soldiers.

Harsh barracks with no recreational facilities left them prey to the attractions of liquor shops, gambling places and brothels.

The plight of these men was seen and recognized by Elsie Sandes, a young woman from Tralee in County Kerry. As a child she had played with Kitchener; as an adult she had the confidence of generals; but she had a heart to care for the serving soldiers and they in response gave their hearts to her.

Elsie had already begun to work among soldiers stationed in Tralee, but on visiting Cork she had seen even greater need and misery occasioned by young men of the garrison at a loose end in the city with some money and much time. After much prayer and effort, in June 1877 she set up in South Mall, Cork, in a plain unfurnished room with bad drains, the first of what was to become a world-wide institution—the Sandes Soldiers' Homes—which still carries on its ministry of love and caring. Later she saw other Homes established in Ireland at Ballykinlar, the Glen of Imaal and on the Curragh, the last mentioned continuing to serve the Irish Army after Independence. Through those early years of the Afghan and Boer wars, and into the even grimmer years of the First World War, Elsie Sandes was to receive many simply written testimonies from soldiers thanking her for a warm homely place and for telling them of the Lord.

Elsie Sandes also gave the use of her rooms in Cork as a meeting place for the newly started Young Men's Christian Association which was founded in London some years earlier and established in Cork by local men in 1886. The cause prospered and within six years they were able to invite D. L. Moody to lay the foundation stone of their new building and halls in Marlboro Street. This he did on 16

September 1892, when he was guest of honour at a lunch.

Young Tommy Hammond was among those who must have eagerly awaited the opening of their very own building. The Annual Report of 1890 lists him as T. Hammond, paying two shillings annual subscription. His progress can be traced in these Annual Reports: Joint Secretary of the Juniors, 1890 and 1891; Secretary of the Evangelisation Conference, 1894; Hon. Secretary of the Junior Department, 1894-95, and on the Gymnasium Committee 1895. Indeed the milestones of his life can be traced in the Minute Books of the Cork 'YM' until the day in 1961 when, on hearing of his death some ten thousand miles away in Australia, the members stood in silent tribute.

The Protestant community in Cork was more numerous then. Emigration, the withdrawal of various English institutions in the 1920s and losses through mixed marriages, have since quartered it. This, coupled with the fact that people were less passive in their entertainments than now, meant that the facilities at the 'YM' were much in demand. Membership, including associates, was over four hundred for many years.

The Association was virtually a little world in itself, where members of the Protestant minority could meet and socialise safe from unwelcome involvement with the majority—as much a matter of necessity as of choice in view of the strong Roman Catholic action on mixed marriages. Lists of suitable accommodation were kept for inspection, the Reading Rooms were open from 10 a.m. to 10 p.m. (although the Secretary had instructions to black out the horse racing results before the newspapers were left in the Rooms!). Apart from these censored papers at least twenty periodicals were available, such as *The British Workman, The Irish Textile Journal* and *The Cyclist*. Shorthand classes were 'pursued vigorously', and musical evenings were often held.

In its leaflets, the Association boasted of 'well fitted lavatories and excellent cycle stables'. Indeed cycling was enjoying great popularity as a means of transport and recreation. Machines with names which evoked solid values like 'The Ormonde' or 'The Girder' could be hired or purchased in nearby Tuckey Street. Bands of cyclists would set off from the 'YM' to local harbourside attractions such as Trebolgan and Fota. Nor were they all young men, for girls were also wheeling their way to greater freedom. The enthusiasm for cycling was harnessed to zeal for evangelism and a Cycling Tract Band was formed, although the impression is given that older members were not altogether happy lest the call of the open road became dominant.

Tommy Hammond took a full part in all these things. He did a little boxing, and being on the Gymnasium Committee he made request to the General Committee for boxing gloves for the boys. The request was turned down! He organised debates, the result of one of which stands on record as forty-five *for* to five *against* the motion that young men should attend the theatre. To his written report of this he added a rider (a trait of his): 'two who voted for the motion have decided after careful consideration that they were wrong in their ideas.'[5] The forceful debater of greater issues in the life of the church in Dublin and in Sydney was already learning his craft!

While mind and body were catered for, the Association did not fail in its primary function. With a healthy balance 'normal' and 'spiritual' programmes were well integrated. A full programme of prayer meetings, Bible studies and evangelistic services kept the title Young Men's *Christian* Association a reality. The work was a spiritual work, the concern was genuine and the standards were high.

As well as providing a centre for fellowship for keen local believers from a variety of backgrounds the Association was host to many whose names are still respected: Grattan Guinness from the missionary side of the brewing family and father-in-law of Hudson Taylor; William Pennefather; George Grubb of Tipperary; Griffith Thomas and A. T. Pierson.

Whether they were locals or visitors, speakers pressed home the same message: God's holiness, man's lost condition and inability to change himself, the folly of his selfish ways, the necessity of regeneration, and the assurance of forgiveness based on the completed work of Christ only. They showed from the Bible that God's grace was free and his love everlasting. They called on those listening to repent and to accept God's way of justification, assured of the promise of the Holy Spirit to make them new in Christ. It was a clear Christ-centred message calling men and women from their sins into a direct relationship with Christ without any intermediary. It made a lasting impact in the lives of those who responded in faith.

JOHN McNAY

One of the young Christian men of those days was John McNay, about whose family we will hear later. He devoted himself to the boys in the YMCA and was popular with them and with their parents. He was in the family boot and shoe business (whose premises are now the Trustee Savings Bank in North Main Street) and many a customer in the shop would say 'won't you look after my boy Mr McNay?'

McNay's family sometimes worried that he was letting the business decline because of his devotion to Christian work. He led Bible studies, took lads on excursions, the Keswick Convention among them. He always stood up for them before the General Committee. In the summer of 1904 he contracted a fever which eventually took his life when he was still only in his mid-forties. 'His work was owned of God to the conversion of many a lad' read the YM's tribute to him.[6] And so it was. The circle of boys round John McNay spread out from Cork and its widening ripples have continued. John Rainsbury whose children were teachers and missionaries was one of his circle. So were the Wood brothers, sons of a hatter, forebears of Bishop M. A. P. Wood; together they went on to start the National Young Life Campaign and to write many books.

Another boy, George Bird, stayed in Cork, found work in the City of Cork Steam Packet Company, and for forty years carried on the work of the Association, so that for generations of Cork people his name was synonymous with the YMCA.

Bird was a quiet, even austere man, who, having lost his first love to another in those early cycling days, never married. Deeply spiritual, he often took out his small pocket New Testament and, whether in the building or on an outing would, on the spot, bring a young man's attention to a verse, invariably drawing three points from it. In later life when writing his own story for the Faith Mission, George Bird had not forgotten the part played by John McNay:

When I was about thirteen years of age a school friend introduced me to the Cork YMCA. The Association had a Junior department whose leader was John McNay, a son of pious Scottish Presbyterian parents. A keen soul-winner, he led many lads, including myself to Christ.[7]

George Bird and Tommy Hammond were life-long friends. Whenever Bird heard of Hammond's intention to return to Cork on a visit he would be there staking his claim to talk to him first. Yet they approached Christ as centre from opposite sides. Bird, quieter and introspective, dwelt more on the 'inner life' and his theology was mildly Arminian in ethos. Hammond was more robust intellectually and doctrinally and was more often found explaining the basis of his faith rather than talking about his own experience. There is a hint that George Bird was disappointed that his more famous friend did not write 'devotional' material. Yet he admired him greatly and in a pot-pourri scrap book, among general news items, poems, photographs and illustrations, he carefully kept news cuttings of Hammond's advancement and travels.

CONVERSION

Tommy Hammond was also one of the McNay group and within that context he was converted to a living faith in Jesus Christ. Exactly how this happened is not clear. He was a careful thinker and it is certain that he did not just 'fall' into belief, not even for John McNay. He could not consciously pin-point a particular time as the moment of re-birth, but he knew he had been brought into new life in Christ. His later writings reflect this: 'Conversion is an experience quite definite, even though the time of conversion or the circumstances are not present definitely in consciousness.'[8]

One clue survives in Cork to throw some light on how it may have happened. A remarkable Australian evangelist, a woman of Jewish birth, Emily Baeyertz[9] visited the Cork YMCA, during the first week of May 1892, as part of a world preaching tour. When she was leaving a testimony meeting was held to give members an opportunity to recount what God had done for them either during the visit or earlier. A page in the Minute Book is given over to record the occasion and about twenty names are listed each one followed by a word or two at most: 'Blessing' or 'Salvation' or 'General Testimony'. Only T. Hammond's comment runs to three words: 'Three miserable months'!

Hammond, who would later be known for the erudition of his mind, obviously experienced a prolonged internal struggle as intellect, will and feelings came to the truth. Young Tommy had had a sense of conviction of sin for some time and had come to assurance of his salvation in Christ prior to the visit of Mrs Baeyertz. Yet in the light of twenty-five fruitful years service in Australia her visit to Ireland just at this time is an interesting link with Tommy's future sphere of service.

STREET PREACHING

Any uncertainty as to how or when Hammond's conversion took place soon slips into the background, eclipsed by the readiness with which he took up the task of commending his Lord to others. Although he was only about fifteen he began to take his place in open-air gospel meetings under the leadership of George Williams.

These meetings in Cork in the 1890s achieved some notoriety and the right to hold them became embroiled in the Home Rule politics of the day. Open-air preaching in

Ireland was never a matter of polite curiosity in any case; until the 1960s heckling and abuse were common and mob violence an ever-present threat. Evangelists were often driven out of provincial towns.

It was not unknown for such actions to be orchestrated by a parish priest. Stories are numerous; in Mullingar in the Midlands a peaceful meeting was turned into a rout by a priest telling the people, 'beat them out of it, they are paid proselytisers'. The disrupters were equipped on that occasion with a trumpet and drum and the bystanders were on their knees singing 'Faith of our Fathers'. Richard Hobson, later a leading Liverpool clergyman and close friend of Bishop J. C. Ryle, told of his days as a colporteur in County Louth when some evangelists were so manhandled that they had to be hospitalised.[10] In Cork Mrs Ainley, a rector's wife, was hit on the head with a stone at an open air meeting on the Marina and never fully recovered.

In his small booklet *Memories Crowd Upon Me* (the substance of a talk given in London in 1948), Hammond described how detachments of armed police would arrive by train in Cork on Saturday evenings in anticipation of riots at 'the preaching'. Much of the centre of Cork is built on an island in the River Lee and a few speakers were thrown into the ever convenient river.

Out of those tumultuous events comes a story about Hammond that has gone around the world and can be met in many versions. It is best told in his own words:

Street preaching was a very riotous undertaking. You required to be young and you required to be very active if you were going to carry on street preaching in Cork in those days. I earned notoriety under the name of 'The Boy Hammond'. I was one of the youngest of the group. On one occasion in the street preaching a section of the mob seized me by the shoulders, and the police, seeing that I was in danger, rushed forward and dragged me by the legs, and I found myself suspended between earth and heaven. Then the police drew their batons and whacked at the knuckles of the men who were holding me by the shoulders, and brought me back to safety. In Sydney a lady, one of the mid-Victorians—they are more Victorian there than they are here—said to me; 'Now, Mr Hammond, what were your thoughts when you were in that terrible position ?' I said, 'If you really want to know I will tell you; but you will be astonished.' 'I would really like to know ' she said. 'Well, my thoughts were—I wonder whether the buttons will hold !'[11]

JOHN O'KEEFE

Another incident from the same days, tinged with pathos rather than humour, gives a glimpse of the often unseen repercussions of street preaching. Hammond was preaching in the street in Cork; the crowd was restive and in an ugly mood; again police were in attendance. One young man broke through the crowd and, snatching Hammond's Douay Testament from him, began to set it alight. Hammond could only say before the push of people separated them: 'That is the Word of God you are burning and what's more it is your own version'.[12]

This confrontation would have merged into a hundred others, but, years later when Hammond was in Dublin he was approached by a worker with the Connellan Mission whom he knew well. The man, whose name was John O'Keefe, explained his predicament: he was in poor health and his doctor suggested that a drier climate was his only hope of recovery. He asked Hammond if he could recommend him to an Australian bishop. Hammond said he knew Bishop Langley, a Tipperary man, and he would recommend O'Keefe to him as a catechist.

There was, however, a further complication, as O'Keefe then went on to explain. He had been brought up a Roman Catholic and had been converted; but he had never really joined any church since. Would Hammond officially 'receive' him into the Church? Hammond agreed, but explained that as a matter of policy he never 'received' people without hearing their own explanation of why they wished to become church members

Only then was an amazing coincidence unveiled as O'Keefe described how he had once tried to break up a meeting by burning the speaker's book, and how the speaker had said that it was the Word of God he was burning. The words had burned into his soul and he had been driven to read the Scriptures for himself, leading to his conversion. Preacher and erstwhile heckler realized they were meeting again.

O'Keefe emigrated to Australia before the First World War, and died there while still a young man, but not before he had been instrumental in giving spiritual help to many in his work as a catechist. He is buried in a neglected grave in White Hills Cemetery, Bendigo, Victoria, among both fellow Irishmen and Chinese who had gone there in gold rush days. When in Australia on his first visit Hammond made a point of visiting the grave.

On that same Australian visit Hammond also spoke at a meeting in the Gold Hall. There he was approached by a man with a remarkable story. The man had lived in Bendigo and had been addicted to drink. Again and again O'Keefe had spoken to him about it, but to no avail. Then the man moved up into the bush in the search for gold and lived out a lonely life in a shack; he slid further into a world of beer and spirits, punctuated only by occasional visits from O'Keefe in his horse-drawn buggy. One day as he lay in his shack surfacing from a bad bout of delirium tremens this man became dimly conscious of O'Keefe by his bed pleading with God for his soul. That settled the matter for him. He said to Hammond, 'and that's why I'm here today a sober man and a Christian'. All from the street preaching in Cork!

QUESTIONS ABOUT STREET PREACHING
On one occasion the street preaching in Cork became a topic of discussion in the House of Commons. One of the leading open-air speakers was George Williams, a former paymaster in the old Royal Irish Constabulary. He had been pensioned off because of arthritis in his hands. Tim Healy, later first Governor General of the Irish Free State, was under pressure to raise the matter of street preaching, although he himself was reluctant to do so, knowing the issue was really one of free speech.

Healy set out to draw attention to the issue through George Williams' position. In a parliamentary question he asked the Chief Secretary why Williams was released from duties. The answer was given that because of arthritis he was unfit for 'clerical duties'. To this Healy put the supplementary question: 'If Mr. George Williams is unfit for *clerical* duties will the Chief Secretary inform the House how it is that he *preaches* every Sunday evening on the streets of Cork? . . . [Laughter].'[13]

It is worth considering why people engaged in preaching in the open air, especially when it antagonised others. What did it achieve? It took courage to face ridicule, the misunderstanding of friends, often the censure of family and the apathy of fellow church members, quite apart from actual street violence or the threat of it. Certainly there was no material gain in it and the number of converts directly resulting from open-air work was depressingly small.

In the Irish situation of the time, those who became believers invariably had to leave home, and often country, because of persecution. Protestants were barely tolerated in the dominant Roman Catholic ethos of the time; 'turncoats' certainly were not. They were 'denounced from the altar', which was tantamount to a sentence of social boycott. Consequently an evangelist did not have the on-going encouragement of the fellowship and support of those whom he had seen turn to Christ.

In fact it was churches in England, America and Australia that tended to benefit from the exodus of converts from Ireland. There must be many Christians in other countries who unknowingly owe a debt which, under God, can be traced back to Irish open-air preaching. But the small body of Irish evangelists, augmented by those who came to Ireland to share their work, kept preaching. Love for God and compassion for their fellow-countrymen motivated them, and the honourable tradition of taking the gospel into the open air, where people were, inspired them.

One thing these faithful evangelists did achieve: they 'held the line'. Like soldiers in some contested salient they guarded the freedom to proclaim the gospel against complete encirclement by darkness. Those who follow today and enjoy greater freedom in the Republic of Ireland owe much to those who took their stand for the gospel on Irish streets.

RAILWAY CLERK AND MARRIAGE

It is possible that from soon after his conversion Hammond wanted to study for the ministry. There is even a hint that he felt attracted to the Presbyterian ministry. But in view of his family circumstances study had to be deferred. At the age of thirteen he took a post as a clerk with the Cork, Bandon and South Coast Railway, a small but distinguished company which served city, town and the scattered communities of West Cork. Labour troubles affected the Railway, and, as a junior clerk, young Tommy Hammond was sometimes in an invidious position. Being considered 'staff' he had to carry out company orders which occasionally involved him driving a horse-drawn wagon round Cork city to circumvent the strikers' tactics. Later he moved to the Great Southern Railway and worked in the engineering office, to the relief, it is said, of some of his former fellow employees who felt uncomfortable with his zealous Christian faith.

But young T. C. Hammond's heart was not in the work and he and the company agreed to part. Asked, years later, what would have happened him if he had not entered Christian work, he replied that he probably would have become a station master.

To complete the Cork part of Hammond's life we must run briefly ahead of the main story. This busy schedule of work, active YMCA involvement and street preaching had still room for one more dimension in the small and modest person of Margaret McNay, a sister of John McNay.

The McNay family came from Glasgow, Scotland. The chronicle of their journey by slow stages from Glasgow to Cork mile-stoned by the births of their children is recorded in an old two-volume family Bible. Two children were born in Scotland, one of whom died, but not before her winsome looks were recorded in a painting. John was born in Limerick, Margaret in Nenagh, County Tipperary and the youngest in Cork. More than his own family, the McNays provided Tommy with warmth and companionship.

The relationship between Hammond and Margaret McNay deepened. She was older than he and gave stability to his enthusiastic nature. Later, when he went to Dublin to study, he always found his way back to the McNay home in Bridge Street, Cork or followed her to Glasgow if she was holidaying with relatives. Good friends in Dublin during his student days remarked on his constancy for the girl 'down the country'. But he had to make his way and be able to provide a home for them in Dublin before they could marry. They were engaged for six years before the wedding took place in the Summer of 1906.

Hammond's niece, then only a child of five, remembered the excitement,[14] though to her it was only 'fuss'. A number of visits between the families were made. Mrs Hammond senior, a very small woman of quaint, almost forbidding aspect, found that walking across the city and climbing the stairs of the Bridge Street home would leave her breathless. Behind a book in a bookcase a small flask of brandy was hidden, which in that home was, no doubt, 'for medicinal use'. The niece, brusquely called 'child', would be sent downstairs for 'a glass for Mrs Hammond'.

The same niece also remembers how, on the evening before the wedding, she was puzzled by the fact that the best china was set out! The wedding was in Shandon Church, the sound of whose famed bells is the possession of all Cork people. The 'breakfast' was in the McNay home, not far away. The bride wore a navy blue silk dress with rows of lace, but also endured a gumboil. The niece was carried by her uncle Tom on his shoulders, legs adangle, while he went singing round the house. The honeymoon was in Switzerland.

In Hammond's own immediate family circle there was at least one mixed marriage; and after his father's death, he, his mother and two sisters had lived briefly with an aunt who was a Roman Catholic. She and her agnostic husband, a dentist, were fond of debate and discussion and Hammond tells us how he learned to defend himself from their two-pronged attacks. He soon could give answers and his young mind was sharpened in debate. He tells how years later when men would meet with problems in the Bible or theology: 'I'd somewhat egotistically say: "that's nothing! My uncle-in-law raised those questions with me when I was ten years of age."'[15]

His older brother, James Henry, came under Roman Catholic influence, possibly in England, and joined the Christian Brothers. He became a teacher in Dublin and Kilrush before going to the house of his order at Kells, County Meath about the time the Brothers moved to Bective Street. It was not an ideal location for in class the teachers had to compete with the noise of a sawmill next door. James Hammond managed to overcome this and had the reputation of being a good and effective teacher. In 1890, when he was only twenty-seven, he died what the order described as an 'edifying death' cared for by the Mercy nuns.[16]

By and large Hammond was reticent to speak about his own family and never mentioned his brother; but two casual remarks in later life reveal his hidden scars. To one audience in Dublin he confided that it was for 'personal reasons' that he had involved himself in the Roman contro-versy. On another occasion in Mullingar when a pharisaical Protestant had boasted that he 'hadn't a drop of papist blood in his veins' Hammond passed it off with the com-ment: 'Well not all of us can say that '.

A TRAINEE AT THE IRISH CHURCH MISSIONS

The daily tallying of tickets sold and the arranging of Cattle Specials for Fair Days were not to be Tommy Hammond's life-work. He was already familiar with the activities of the Irish Church Missions (ICM), a Church of Ireland mission principally to Roman Catholics. Various members of the mission staff had regularly spoken at meet-ings in the YM and the ICM also had a Day School in Cork. They had a reputation for dynamic work and ran training courses for evangelists.

Thus in the autumn of 1895, along with two other young Cork people, Hammond applied to enter the Train-ing School in the Mission Headquarters at Dublin. One applicant, a girl, was turned down, the other whose name was McCarthy, although apparently not up to the Mission's usual standard, was allowed in because he was from a Roman Catholic background. Interestingly this candidate's address was 'care of' the Rev Ainley, whose wife had been struck by a stone at an open-air. Hammond, then living at 3 Dryden Place, Ballinlough Road, was also accepted. Somebody, not knowing that the latest candidate was one day to be Superintendent with a name that was to be syn-onymous with the ICM, entered him as T. B. Hammond.

The three-year course was partly in general education, with subjects like Grammar, Geography, Euclid and Singing, but mostly of a theological nature, including the study of Old and New Testament books, the Thirty-Nine Articles and the 'Roman Controversy'. Finally classes were given in applied subjects like Reading and School Management. Hammond was allowed to 'neglect' singing!

The result of one of his tests is not without interest:[17]

Old Testament	10	Prayer Book	10	Geography	7
39 Articles	9	History	9	Reading	7
Controversy	7	Arithmetic	8	Dictation	9
The 100 Texts	8	Grammar	8	Writing	6.5
		School management	5		

Hammond's name is often cited as the author of *The Hundred Texts*, the well-known reference work on points of theology disputed between Protestantism and Roman Catholicism. It is often assumed that he originated this work as a system of teaching in the Roman Controversy. In fact, as can be seen from his exam results, the selection of texts pre-dated Hammond. They had been in use since the mid-nineteenth century and Henry Fishe, who was Superintendent when Hammond was a trainee, had published them in booklet form in groups of ten with notes.

Some readers will not fail to note that the lowest marks of the future Principal of Moore College, Sydney were in School management! He finished the course and 'passed' with the recommendation that he should be a Scripture Reader, a colporteur-evangelist . . . but not a teacher!

ITINERATING

Trainees were sent out itinerating with an experienced worker. Thus from 1897 until 1899 Hammond spent blocks of six to eight weeks evangelising in fairs and markets in counties Tyrone, Donegal, Galway, Limerick, Tipperary and Cork, preaching, selling literature and giving 'magic lantern' [slide] shows.

Cookstown in County Tyrone, which he described as 'a strong presbyterian village about a mile long and eighty yards wide, like Jerusalem "compactly built together"', is the setting for two stories which Hammond told, both illustrative of Irish religious life. The first concerns a simple plain Roman Catholic woman:

One day an old woman came up to me and she said: 'Is there anything about holy water in that book of ours?' 'There is, madam,' I replied. 'I will show it to you'—I want to illustrate the fact that Mission workers were alert—'Here it is' and I read to her the story of the soldier who pierced the side of our Saviour, from whence flowed out blood and water. I said: 'That is the only holy water mentioned and it is the only holy water that ever did anyone any good!'

Hammond goes on to tell how she bought the book, (presumably a Douay New Testament). The next year, when he was in the area again she came to him to tell him how she and her husband would read a chapter every night before retiring and that she was trusting in the blood and water that flowed from the side of the Son of God.

The other story he told to illustrate 'unblushing antinomianism', as he called it. It is a true reflection of an aberration of Christianity sadly common in Ulster:

Many years ago I was selling Testaments and preaching in . . . Cookstown. When I stopped speaking a man lurched towards me. Perhaps I should say he was not a Presbyterian. In a voice thickened by his free use of liquor, he said 'Are you saved?' 'Did you hear me preach?' I asked. 'Och aye' he said 'But mony's the man who preaches who is not saved.' 'Well now' I said 'If I have been lying to the folk around for half an hour, do you think it would bother me to add just one wee one more for your benefit? Anyway, you're drunk, man.' 'Aye' he said, 'I know I'm drunk, but I'm saved all the same'.

Two further stories come from his experiences in Thurles in Tipperary:

We were working at Thurles fair when a girl came back to our stall and said 'Here's yer auld book, the priest has just told me its a fraud.' I thought the incident was closed but some pig drovers egged on the crowd and as they jostled us, getting more and more hostile, I said to my fellow-worker, 'We can do no more. Let's pack up.' We hurried up the street followed by a shouting mob and made a dive for a pub [to take refuge from the pursuing mob]. The publican stood with his arms across the threshold. There was no help for it. I drew out and caught him under the chin with my fist. He fell back and we dived in after him. I was considering what would happen next when the calm voice of a sergeant of police broke the silence. 'That fella struck me' shouted the publican. 'This is a public hostelry' I replied. 'Wait now, wait now' says the sergeant 'what's your name?' Anxious to be strictly correct I said slowly, 'Thomas Chatterton . . . I got no further. Quick as lightning he asked 'Are ye any relation to the Vice-Chancellor?' [Sir Hedge Eyre Chatterton]. 'I am' I replied. To my surprise he took the publican aside. I could only hear fragments of their conversation. 'These young men do be religious like'.

His behaviour on another occasion, Hammond admitted, might not have been altogether ethical but it was certainly effective. He was trying to sell a Douay New Testament to a farmer who was reluctant to accept its authenticity. He pointed to the *imprimatur* of Dr Tracey, and showed the man another Douay for comparison. Still doubt lingered. So,

Almost in despair I pointed to a sheet at the front of the book and read 'This edition is printed from the stereotype plates of Coyne's original edition'. 'Look at that, Sir,' I said, 'I need not explain to a man of your intelligence the meaning of stereotype. That is a guarantee of the genuineness of the book.' He bought it.[18]

In the Mission Training School Hammond gained a thorough grounding in Scripture and in Anglican theology. He was always grateful for this, because it proved to be an unshakeable foundation for his life's work. He was also well schooled in the intricacies of the Roman Controversy, and trained to expose the illogicalities and contradictions of more sophisticated Catholicism. This was to be his forte during his years as Mission Superintendent, as we shall see.

Over and above the content of his training, its enduring value lay in the methods he learned. The students were trained to know, quote, and always verify their references. This was taken very seriously. Today it might be considered pedantic and over scrupulous, but it made for accuracy and certainty. Many an opponent was silenced and many a point thus carried. This was the reason why Hammond was feared and respected by the Roman Catholic Church. He could (and did) put his finger on false information and expose non-sequiturs and demolish slovenly presented arguments.

It is said that once while Hammond was in London he wandered to Hyde Park Corner and was drawn to listen to a speaker from the Catholic Evidence Guild. After one particularly bold statement he interrupted. 'You're wrong' he said 'and if you go to the British Museum Reading Room

. . .' and then he proceeded to refer to a particular book by its shelf location number, title and page '. . . you will see where you are wrong'. The speaker was so deflated he mumbled to a quick close and left.

Throughout his life, until his last decade, Hammond enjoyed a prodigious and photographic memory. He could read a book through and recall accurately statements in it, often remembering the very page or, at least, whether his quotation was on the left-hand or right-hand page.

The Mission was a hard school with little concession to personal wishes, but it was a happy place where staff and students were drawn close to one another by the rough and tumble of evangelistic work. Hammond's good humour and warm nature made him popular. The youth from Cork was changing into a fine young man, well able to hold his own in Dublin.

But Hammond did not go on at that stage to join the staff of the Mission. His intention was to seek ordination in the Church of Ireland. The turn of the twentieth century saw him poised to enter Trinity College, Dublin.

4

A Parish In Dublin

Tommy Hammond was eventually able to undertake a University education as a preparation for ordination. With the help of a small legacy, some savings, the possibility of giving 'grinds' (private tuition to students preparing for examinations), and by keeping his expenses to a minimum, he could apply to Trinity College, Dublin, and register for the specially tailored course of Divinity dovetailed into Arts taken by Anglican ordinands.

A long hard road lay ahead. The small circle of sympathetic Cork evangelicals and fellow-workers in the Mission had to be exchanged for a wider world where his faith would be exposed to critical analysis and testing. Such testing could shatter a man's faith and leave him with only a moralistic religion which any humanist could match, or it could make him unshakeable in his convictions for life.

As part of the need for economy at every turn, Hammond availed himself of a regulation by which it was possible to study outside College and then present oneself for First Year examinations. Accordingly he did not actually enter the urbane world of College life until January 1900, still six years before his marriage.

Trinity College in those days was an uncrowded, unhurried island of manners and customs already left far behind by the city which surrounded it. There were no women students as yet, Greek and Latin were still important and technology was only beginning to gain a foothold. More particularly the Divinity School still reflected sound biblical scholarship. The largely evangelical nature of the nineteenth century Church of Ireland was well represented among students and professors. Even those who were not openly evangelical were 'low church' and took the Bible as their reliable authority. The emphasis was on the text of Scripture.

It was not possible to study in Trinity at that time without being brought into very close working knowledge of the text of Scripture both in English and in the original Hebrew and Greek. Painstaking effort ensured that students first and foremost knew what Scripture said, by contrast with later generations when young men with little more than a Sunday-school knowledge of the Bible were thrown into the maze of critical scholarship and liberal theology.

Good work on the elucidation of the biblical text, its exposition and defence had been done by men who taught in the Divinity School. T. K. Abbott published works on biblical manuscripts and wrote commentaries. W. K. Hobart published a detailed examination of Luke's writing, *The Medical Language of St Luke* (1882), proving him to be a medical man; if somewhat over-refined the work is still of value and has been frequently cited. Other scholars from the School were J. D. Newport White, J. Paterson Smyth, Dr John Gwynn, J. H. Bernard and A. H. McNeile. But towering above them all was George Salmon.

Before turning to theology, Salmon's scholarly reputation had already been established in mathematics (he was an internationally recognised expert on conic sections). He then brought the same incisive logical mind to divinity and earned the title 'the Hammer of the Germans'. Not that the German theologians felt his blows, for then, as later, conservative contributions to theological scholarship were largely ignored. But his attacks on the liberal critics, in which he augmented the work of scholars like B. F. Westcott of the 'Cambridge School', gave courage and heart to many.

George Salmon's strength was in a common sense loyalty to what was actually there in the text of Scripture rather than to the speculative methodology then gaining popularity among critics. This common sense he could assert with humour, as when he remarked of Synoptic studies: 'These things are worked out with brains not with blue and red pencils'. He demolished another critical hypothesis by suggesting that it would require Paul to have had a private yacht! He also wrote on the Apocrypha, but his best known book is *The Infallibility of the Church* (1888), in which he dealt with Roman claims to infallibility. A well-written work, it remains unanswered. The Divinity School in late Victorian times acted more as counsel for the defence with regard to Scripture than it ever did in the twentieth century.

When Tommy Hammond came to Trinity, Salmon was serving as its Provost. It is unlikely that he was still lecturing then, but his character and scholarship were still dominant and his books continued to be used as textbooks.

Hammond began as a student in History but changed and followed a course in Philosophy, Ethics and Logic. Here the duck to water analogy holds good. All his later work and writings show how fully he benefited from these demanding intellectual disciplines. He developed a well-stocked mind, and sharpened his critical faculties, gaining several University Prizes as he progressed, including the Downes Prize for Extempore Speaking, the Wray Prize in Arts, and finally a Gold Medal in Philosophy.

In College at the same time as Hammond was Geoffrey Studdert Kennedy the beloved, if unorthodox, 'Woodbine Willie', who during the First World War sought to bridge the great gap between clergymen and common soldiers and won a hearing for himself in the trenches. But apart from attending the same lectures it is unlikely that Hammond and he had much in common.

It was different in the case of another mercurial Irishman, Everard Digges LaTouche. This son of a distinguished and wealthy Huguenot family was little short of a prodigy. By the age of twenty-seven he was a Doctor of Laws and had written two books: *Christian Certitude* (on apologetics) and *The Person of Christ in Modern Thought,* in which he incisively analysed and refuted the continental writers of various sceptical lives of Christ. The latter book (to which Hammond contributed an appendix on the subconscious) was the substance of the Donnellan Lectures which he gave in 1912.

The friendship between these two men went much deeper than mere literary co-operation. It was Hammond who, as a fellow-student, had pointed the agnostic Digges LaTouche to faith in Christ. Like an expensive firework that shoots skyward for a few brilliant moments, La Touche's career took him to Australia where he was for a short time, in turn, a country rector, a diocesan missioner and a lecturer in Moore College. Then, against the advice of his friends and his bishop, having failed to get a post as a chaplain at the outbreak of the Great War, he enlisted as a combatant in the Australian Forces. Two Turkish bullets at Suvla in the Gallipoli Campaign ended his earthly life on 8 August 1915.[1]

For Tommy Hammond theological training was only a means to an end (his heart was in Cork). He took little part in the social life of the College, although he worked well and conscientiously. He stayed with the Cole family whose son, Alan, he baptised. Little did Hammond know that Alan would later serve with him at Moore College, Sydney and himself become a distinguished New Testament scholar.[2]

Later he stayed in rented 'rooms' in the College in the building known as *The Rubrics* because of its red brick veneer. This arrangement was convenient for his 'grinding' work. He was a good 'grinder'. Robert Tate, later Sir Robert (an honour gained for his defence of Trinity in the 1916 Rising) having come over from Cambridge to sit for a Trinity Fellowship, went to Hammond for help with his 'grinds'. Afterwards as a Fellow of the College he said, 'I owe more than I can say to Hammond for grinds'.[3] An academic career in Philosophy or Theology would certainly have come relatively easily to Hammond.

SAINT KEVIN'S PARISH
While Tommy was completing his studies in 1903 and preparing to graduate, Phineas Hunt, the first Rector of St Kevin's Church on the South Circular Road, Dublin, was looking out for a good curate to help him in the heavy work of the parish. The 'new' church had been built in 1888 to meet the need of the growing number of improving artisans, craftsmen, Guinness Brewery workers and small business men moving out of inner city areas, a trend which

increased further after the introduction of electric trams in 1896. In this mobility lay some of the seeds of its later demise as those it served kept moving further out.

The Parish of St Kevin's had origins going back to medieval Dublin, and until the 1920s the clergy continued to conduct services in 'old' St Kevin's in Kevin Street With his Vestrymen (the elected leadership committee of the congregation, at that stage all male), Hunt had held a series of meetings to discuss whether the parish could afford a curate. When the question of salary had been almost settled, he told them that he had 'interviewed many applicants for the position . . . and hoped to settle the matter by the end of the year.'[4]

The appointment was subsequently made and T. C. Hammond was ordained deacon on 20 December 1903. He preached his initial sermon that evening on 1 Corinthians 9:16, 'Woe is unto me if I preach not the gospel.'

The Rector, Phineas Hunt, was now much less able to sustain his former ministry. He had been a curate assistant in Thurles in famine times, and had eye trouble. Increasingly the burden fell on Hammond. He had all the usual tasks of a curate, including working with the youth and parish visiting which, with the popularity of St Kevin's, took him all over the city.

The young curate also had his share of the less pleasant aspects of parish ministry, such as telling a temporary organist that he was by no means to assume that the post would be his if the regular organist, then in his nineties, died, or placating a local doctor who stormed out of a meeting when he failed to be re-elected to office. Sextons were a constant problem, a difficulty often created by church members treating them as personal servants, compounded by the notorious inability of even the saintliest to please everybody in a church. Again Hammond had to act as the mouthpiece for both the Rector and the Vestry.

Somewhat unwisely, he was also made church treasurer, a position better held by a lay person. The previous treasurer had created such confusion that good stewardship was restored only when Hammond started the accounts again 'on a proper footing'. Even this did not prevent the former treasurer from accusing him of 'trickery', a charge he had to withdraw.

By the end of Hammond's first year as a curate he was already chairing meetings of the Vestry in place of the ailing Rector. Now a new vigour came to the meetings, more subjects of a theological nature arose and a new reality asserted itself. Until then the minutes of the Vestry meetings were kept in what could only be described as 'minutese', a very proper but anaemic English full of set phrases and dull formulas. That also changed. On one occasion, for example a sexton was dismissed for 'unsatisfactory behaviour', to which formula Hammond added and initialed the words: 'that is to say he pawned the church silver . . . TCH'.[5]

The whole ethos of the church was evangelical; spiritual progress was made, not so much by inroads into an unsympathetic or uncommitted membership as by sound teaching from the pulpit and by the work of the organisations. There was a very full programme of services, Christian Endeavour, prayer meetings, Sunday schools, hospital services and attendance at open air preaching at Harold's Cross Bridge, together with hefty missionary giving. This made for a well taught, loyal, and active membership who had little need to look elsewhere to spend time or money. In a period of under thirty years St Kevin's church produced fourteen men for the ministry of the Church of Ireland, while churches more favoured and cultivated by the bishops produced none.

RECTOR

In 1910, when Phineas Hunt had finally to resign and seek a lighter parish in County Sligo, few were surprised that the popular and hard-working curate was made rector. In fact he had been that in all but name. There was little need for change, but Hammond, with the relative independence of being rector could now take more part in wider church matters. He had become increasingly well-known as a popular preacher and as a 'sound Protestant'. He wrote to the newspapers, often using his pen in the cause of individuals who were wronged on account of their faith or their convictions. On one occasion he defended the rights of a man who, having worked thirty-eight years for a bookseller, was dismissed because he was seen helping to serve free meals at the Metropolitan Hall: 'Opinions differ as to the wisdom or necessity of the same, but the point is it is a free country.'[6]

But he also wrote on issues of the wider life of the Church and was not slow to write to the press to correct Dr Bernard, then Archbishop King's Professor, later Archbishop of Dublin, on a point of liturgical use. He spoke at meetings of the Anti-Ritualistic Society when churchmen tried to nip resurgent priestcraft in the bud, declaring at one of their meetings (with reference to the ritualists' love of sanctuaries): 'when he wanted to find the Almighty he didn't need the assistance of ropes and gates.'[7]

When the Church of Ireland Bishop of Tuam issued

a leaflet in 1915 which included prayers for the dead, something for which there was a demand following the large number of war bereavements, Hammond took the matter up with the Archbishop in Armagh. Eventually there was a compromise retraction.

Hammond took a particular interest in the Divinity School, realising that it was the source of most of the teaching the ordinary Church of Ireland member was likely to get. As a city rector close to Trinity College and with his theological ability he had his finger on the theological pulse. Small changes in lecturers and text-books signalled a falling away from previous standards. So at his first Easter vestry as rector (1911) a resolution was passed stressing the 'urgent need to reform the teaching imparted in the Divinity School of Trinity College . . . [and to provide] . . . adequate Protestant and Evangelical instruction'.[8]

This resolution was also sent to the press for publication. The next year Hammond took up the same theme in the Dublin Diocesan Synod. This time the issue was more specific. The Divinity School was using a work on the Prayer Book by Procter and Frere which advanced liturgical usages foreign to the Church of Ireland, including the use of sacerdotal vestments.

Professor Newport White, replying for the School, said that they used the book because its scholarship was good and since the School was 'Protestant and Evangelical' there was little danger that any one would be influenced by small peculiarities. As to the vestments mentioned in it: 'he would only read it as he would read a description of the fantastic dress of the natives of Patagonia.'[9] But it was not long before this 'fantastic dress' was being worn in the Church of Ireland!

Hammond pursued his concern for the Divinity School knowing its vital importance. He worked with Dr Montgomery Hitchcock in an effort to make it answerable to the General Synod of the Church, and to ensure that a student going forward for the ministry had an adequate theological training. As things stood the amount of training was at the discretion of the individual ordaining bishop.

When Montgomery Hitchcock brought the matter up in Synod in 1918 it was ruled out of order (*ultra vires*). This was appealed and the case was heard before the Court of the General Synod in January 1919. But now the issue had widened, for at root was the question of the bishops' authority. Hammond prepared a masterly argument and brief for counsel in which he traced various checks and controls on episcopal authority in church history from the time of the Fathers and the Early Councils. This was published as *Authority In The Church*.

The appeal was lost. It foundered on the in-built ambiguity of the Church Constitution drawn up at the Disestablishment in 1869. It laid down that the Church was to be under the control of the General Synod (*i.e.* all its elected members) subject to its episcopal nature (*i.e.* the bishops). That position was workable only until there was a conflict between members and bishops.

Hammond maintained his concern about the School. When a Catholic bishop attacked it, he spoke up in defence of the facts. This, however, was soon forgotten, while his words written in the context of internal controversy endured.

He worked on at parish level and throughout the city. While he disapproved of some religious developments he had an open-mindedness to others and was 'ecumenical' in the truest and best sense of the word. His preaching in the Methodist church in Dolphin's Barn (apparently the first time a rector had occupied a Methodist pulpit in Ireland), was a thing worthy of note in the newspapers of the day. When complaint was made about this he explained that it was within his parish bounds so that he was merely preaching in his own parish! Throughout his life he was often in the same position as other evangelical Anglicans: too Anglican for Baptist and Brethren friends but also too open to 'dissenters' for most Anglicans.

The St Kevin's years were also important family years. In 1906, while still a curate, Hammond had married Margaret McNay. Their four children were born during the years before they left St Kevin's. John, the eldest, was reared and educated by a friend, Miss Kemble, who had been on the ICM staff, and spent most of his life in England. The other three, Thomas Chatterton ('Chat'), Carl and Doris grew up in Dublin and all went to Trinity College.

Outside the home violent upheavals would soon break up the calm surface of Edwardian Dublin. The Transport Strike of 1913, the Great War, the abortive Easter Rising of 1916, the War of Independence and the Civil War (1922-23) came like a series of succeeding thunder storms on a sultry summer day. But in the home there was the warmth and shelter of happy Christian love and healthy intellectual stimulation. Even late in life Chat could remember being brought as a child into his parents' cosy bed to be taught Latin!

The parish had not yet been able to afford a rectory and Hammond rented his own house first at number 40 in Dublin's famed Synge Street, birthplace of George Bernard Shaw, and then at 10 Stamer Street.

It should be understood that throughout his ministry at St Kevin's, Hammond would not have thought of himself as anything but a loyal citizen of King and Empire. So did thousands of Dubliners; it was normal. King Edward and his Queen had paid a visit to Dublin in 1911 and were warmly welcomed and when the call to defend the Empire came in 1914 it is estimated that sixteen per cent of men of military age in Leinster volunteered to serve.

Holidays were taken occasionally in Wales but usually in County Wicklow where the family had the use of a rectory at Ballinacor near Aughrim (pronounced 'Ockram'). Even then they were 'on duty' for their father would bring down from the city someone who required help or needed to get a break or the opportunity to be with 'a bright family'. The children did not like being 'the bright family', but he would say 'Now come on, we need to show love and help people', and so they would fall in behind their big-hearted father. On holidays he would play games with them like 'a big kid' and cycle with them, leaping on the bicycle from behind in the old-fashioned way learned in Cork, coat tails flying.[10]

Until she died in 1918, Hammond's sister, Mary, devoted herself to the care of her mother. Then Mrs Hammond senior came to live with the family until her death in 1921. Another sister had married a clergyman but had been widowed. Her unruly family were a constant worry and for many years Hammond carried them through one misfortune after another, many of their own making.

When the time came for the Hammonds to leave St Kevin's, the ordinary members expressed their regret at losing a dear pastor and the Vestry recorded their appreciation of his ministry and expressed the trust that 'he be mightily used of God as a soul-winner and to promote and advance Evangelical Truth.'[11] Their trust was not misplaced.

TC always received a warm welcome whenever he returned to St. Kevin's. But one matter in relation to the parish accounts followed him. When he left the Poor Fund was £119 overdrawn. Asked about this he replied that the Fund was 'wholly inadequate' for the crying needs of the parish. He himself had dipped deeply into his own pocket and expected the same of the parish. Indeed, years later when he went to Australia he left a small fund in the Ulster Bank in Camden Street for his old retainers and arrived in Australia without money in hand.

Hammond was succeeded in St Kevin's by Richard Bird, a quieter but godly man, with a great knack of involving himself in every facet of his parishioners' lives. He had recently returned from the War where he had won the DSO for bringing in wounded men under fire and had been a prisoner of war ('a guest of the Kaiser' as he put it) for a time in Karlsruhe. Bird was from Ballydulea in Cork and a relative of Hammond's friend George Bird.

During the short vacancy between rectors a member of the vestry pushed through a resolution that gained some passing fame. As a result, the clergy of St Kevin's were to ask any visiting clergyman not to wear a cassock. A notice to that effect was put up in a prominent place. Sometimes the straws are considered more important than the wind that blows them. Some years later the original wording was mollified by a further resolution expressing the sentiment: 'Sirs, we would see Jesus.' That request was entirely in keeping with the spirit of Hammond's ministry there.

5

At The Irish Church Missions

When the Reverend J. R. Goff indicated that he was going to resign from the position of Superintendent of the Irish Church Missions the Committee had little difficulty in choosing his successor. T. C. Hammond had by now become well known as a stout defender of evangelical Protestantism and as an effective debater. In his time in St Kevin's he had received a number of Roman Catholics into the Church of Ireland. In addition he had been trained by the Mission.

Members of the committee paid a number of visits to discuss matters with him and early in 1919 he succeeded Goff. He was to become the best known Superintendent of the Mission and under him it reached its zenith, unless it is yet to have a greater role in Irish Christian witness. Some years later he was made General Superintendent, so that he was also responsible for the Mission's activities in England involving him in much travel, seeking prayer and financial support.

Hammond led the Mission through times of great bitterness and contention in Ireland set against the background of a triumphalist, intolerant Roman Catholicism. The peculiar position of the Church of Ireland at the time made the Roman question an acute one.

If Hammond were fighting some of the same battles today he would probably have many informed Roman Catholics on his side. It was a time when the evangelical cause in the south of Ireland was under constant verbal and occasionally physical attack from instruments of Catholic action and at the same time was being deserted by friends who were either leaving Ireland in fear of Home Rule or whose ardour was being quenched by Modernism and the effects of misguided biblical criticism. It was, in fact, the last days of old establishment evangelicalism.

Dublin was in tumult. On top of the terrible poverty and wretched conditions that gave it the highest child death-rate in Europe the political pot was coming to the boil. The coolness, if not hostility, with which the Easter Rising in 1916 had been met by the citizens of the city was transformed by the executions of its leaders. It now became a popular cause and patriotic fervour was expressed in a hundred ways. Culture, sport, civic affairs and trade union-ism were all harnessed to the Nationalist cause as never before.

Hammond's first three years in the Mission covered the War of Independence and the Civil War. The British had their home and country to go back to, the nationalists had their country to fight for, but Protestants, mostly Unionist in politics, were left as orphans, cut off from the friends and institutions with whom they had grown up. They were not particularly welcome in the new Irish Free State.

So intense was this feeling that a delegation from the Church of Ireland, including Archbishop Gregg, went to Michael Collins in the early summer of 1922. Collins (1890-1922), was a leading Irish Republican Army (IRA) activist and signatory of the peace treaty in 1921 to end the Anglo-Irish War. The following year he was shot and killed in an ambush in west Cork. Thus, shortly before Collins' death, churchmen were asking him if there was to be any place for them in Ireland. They were bewildered and had a very real sense of being let down by the England their fathers and they had served. They felt abandoned by their fellow Protestants in the north of Ireland, who were satisfied to let their southern friends sink or swim, as they held on to what they had and opted out of involvement in the new Ireland.

Throughout these turbulent years Hammond acted as editor of *The Catholic*, the paper started by Thomas Connellan. His forebodings at the events being acted out around him can be seen in his editorials. Hopes for peaceful and sane solutions were raised only to founder and genuine efforts to negotiate were thwarted by acts of senseless violence on both sides.

During 'the troubles' the roof of the Hammond family home in Stamer Street was used by republican Sinn Fein snipers (pronounced *Shin Fane*). Hammond and his young family were brought, quite literally, into the firing line of British retaliation. His daughter, Doris, tells of being awakened and hurriedly bundled into the corridor while mattresses were put up to the windows. Their father was a reassuring comfort as he occupied their minds by playing with them. When one of the boys complained that he couldn't play 'I spy' in the dark he was told to use his sanctified imagination!

The children often knew real fear since their father was frequently called out to attend to the wounded and, despite their mother's assurances, they would not sleep until they heard him quietly slip in later. Even greater danger lay in the fact that he was being used by both sides as an intermediary. He received messages by surreptitious means.

No one can be so used without risking misunderstanding and it was well known that he was for a time on a 'hit-list'. A nationalist who later became involved in evangelistic work told how Hammond's name came up for 'review'; but he had gained such a reputation for helping people regardless of their religion that action was postponed. On one occasion, whether by accident or on purpose, he was fired at and his sleeve was torn. He never discovered whether it was a poor shot or a warning.

Hammond's own strong feelings surfaced when he spoke at a Congress in London in October 1922, just after the Treaty with England had been signed but while the Civil War still raged. He recognized that English people would not want to hear any more about Ireland:

When we talk about Ireland they meet us with the message of the old woman to the prophet, 'Art thou come to call my sin to remembrance?' He then traced how Jesuits worked after the Reformation to foment division, and how when England got rid of the 'Papal King' (James II): You left us starving behind the walls of Derry; you left us gripping our muskets on the Boyne to keep your back door for you; and to-day you have betrayed your trust . . . and what is the result?. . . Ireland is stained with blood and crime. To-night for aught you and I know, men are groaning in their last agony upon the hills of that land.

And then very significantly for a Unionist he continued:

We will go on and on till this fair land that once honoured the name of the Most High shall once again become the Kingdom of our Lord and of His Christ. In that day we will be content for our portion . . . because we rest not on politicians nor on empires . . .[1]

Nor was this only a matter of feelings and oratory while on a platform in London, for on the ground in Dublin he had to go about his work under constant threat. Asked once whether he ever got threatening letters he replied that he could paper the walls with them. Steel shutters had to be used in the Mission building. The children in the Homes had to be cared for and fed in the midst of Revolution; the Orphanage at Aashleigh in Galway was cut off for months. Nothing was certain.

SEARCH THE SCRIPTURES

The Irish Church Missions headquarters were then situated in large and commanding premises at 5a Townsend Street. (Since demolished, the last service being held in June 1968, it is now the site of College House.) The name was painted on the roof in huge letters and over the door were inscribed the words 'Search the Scriptures'. Earlier the Mission had been in premises further down the street until the building of a loop line by the railway dictated a move. The same words 'Search the Scriptures' had been inscribed on the old building and had remained legible on the demolished remains. This occasioned their being covered up by local people every time there were catholic processions in the area. Hammond took over a full machinery of classes, meetings and services. He made no sudden changes but, from within, motivated and enthused the staff to great efforts.

Under Hammond's supervision were a number of schools, most of which had been started in the nineteenth century with their own committees to run them, but the ICM was responsible for the teaching given. These schools met a real need among the pre-Social Services poor helping the unfortunate child casualties of broken homes and divorces 'Irish style' when the father just took off and started a new life and family in England. They were for many the only hope when accident, sickness or death shattered their fragile family security. Some of the children came as day pupils but many others lived on the premises, having no other home.

In the schools the religious instruction was given by means of the well-tried 'Hundred Texts'. The children were trained to memorise these carefully chosen verses and their biblical references. When a child knew the Hundred Texts he had learned, in fact, 164 verses and a considerable amount of theology covering major Christian doctrines. The teaching was, admittedly, repetitive and unimaginative but it was solid. Generations of Mission children would appreciate a misprint seen in one booklet which called them 'The Hundred Tests'!

Sometimes for visitors a show of answering was arranged. On one occasion, some of the children were taken to England and at a meeting gave a display of their knowledge. One clergyman in the meeting thought it was too good to be true, and suspecting that the children knew which verses were to be asked he requested an opportunity to examine them:

Clergyman: What does Timothy say about the inspiration of Scripture? [Silence] Aha! you don't know that one.
Small Dublin boy: Please Sir, Timothy doesn't say anything about inspiration, but Paul in Second Timothy Chapter three verse sixteen says 'All Scripture is inspired of God . . .'[2]

70

T. C. Hammond also had a team of evangelists and visitors who engaged in direct evangelism throughout Dublin and in the Provinces. This was thankless work carried on against prevailing ignorance, suspicion and hostility. That is well-illustrated by a survival tactic the visitors had to adopt when visiting the tenements which housed many families. The rule was to start on the top floor in order to keep a line of retreat open. One visitor was met at the doorstep with a sword. Even when they offered the Douay New Testament it was slandered as 'a communist book'!

OPEN AIR MEETINGS

A more public form of witness was carried out by regular open air meetings held in prominent city venues such as Abbey Street and Foster Place. These were, by and large, accepted by Dubliners, even if only for their entertainment value, and if a fight broke out, so much the better. Preachers had to steer round the use of the name Jesus, for when it was used the crowd would 'bless' themselves by making the sign of the cross. It was found less disruptive to refer to 'the Saviour' or 'our Lord'.

Dublin people have a very droll wit expressed mostly by their own distinctive way of handling the English language. But the preachers and workers gave as good as they got in the same idiom. The following retorts come from the annals of the work and are found over and over again:

Heckler: Wha'bout Henry d' Eighth?
Reply: What about him? He was to his dying day one of yours, and you're welcome to him!
Heckler: Where was youser religion before Luther?
Reply: Where was your face before you washed it? [This riposte can be traced back to George Salmon]

Heckler: D' ye believe in de sacrifice of de Mass?
Reply: Let me ask you. What does the priest break after conse-cration? {This created a dilemma for the Roman Catholic since if the priest broke *bread* Transubstantiation was not true ... if he supposedly broke *the body of Christ* then the Scripture 'not a bone of him shall be broken' was contradicted}.

Clearly these open-air meetings were no place for the faint hearted or the slow thinking! Once when a bottle was thrown a speaker picked it up saying 'Empty! Like the devil's promises'.

Hammond himself told of a street preacher, who, feeling the meeting was getting out of control largely because of the interjections of a rather tough and toothless old woman, spoke pointedly at her about the dangers of find-ing herself where there would be 'weeping and gnashing of teeth.' To this she retorted: 'Let 'em gnash 'em what has dem to gnash'.

The most common interruption was the frequent, sim-plistic, shouting of the text 'Thou art Peter and upon this rock I will build my church'. The words were believed to end all argument. On one such occasion, when Hammond had been speaking for some time a man came up and star-ing into his face repeated the 'Thou art Peter' formula. But a voice from the crowd dismissed the interruption saying: 'Ah, you're late, Mick, he knocked the bottom out of that one half an hour ago!'[3]

Catholic Action and later the Legion of Mary constantly picketed these meetings. Sometimes they held up a notice saying 'By just standing here you may be committing a Mortal Sin'. Others walked past with their fingers in their ears, and thus became, as the Mission staff put it, 'their own jailers'.

THE 'CONTROS'

To follow up on the work of the street meetings there were widely advertised 'Controversial Meetings' held in the Mission building. Known as the 'Contros' they dealt with subjects connected with the Roman Controversy. Mission policy was always to focus on the heart of the gospel in the street and to discuss controversial matters in the Mission premises. These were often boisterous and rowdy meetings with a leavening of humour. It was here that Hammond shone, and when old Dubliners were asked for recollections of him it was the details of his conducting of these 'Contros' that they remembered best: a packed hall of ordinary Dublin people, a fuggy atmosphere, a number of hecklers and Hammond's sturdy figure on the platform, alone, demolishing all arguments:

Ladies and Gentlemen . . . recently Cardinal Gibbons said . . . but in the year 1590 Cardinal Bellarmine said . . . and in the year 1262 Thomas Aquinas said . . . Well there's something wrong about these contradictions. Infallibility seems to be rather less assured than it has ever been!

Then off Hammond would go into a storm of eloquence about what really mattered in Christian doctrine or church practice if it was 'apostolic'. He would end by explaining the central themes of the gospel and the way of justification by faith.

The hearers did not always follow every point. One man, bewildered by Hammond's references to the Roman Catholic Council of Trent (1545-63), was overheard saying 'Who's this Councillor Trent he talks about?' A woman was heard to say 'I don't care what Mr Hammond says I don't think the Pope is infallible'! The subtleties of his logic were at times beyond them, but they knew that he understood what he was talking about; they also knew that no priest was willing to confront him in public debate.

On one occasion an English visitor was present and was critical of Hammond for the intellectually demanding character of his address to such a 'simple' audience, and particularly for the quotations he was using from Augustine and Tertullian. He was determined to have a word with him about this when the meeting finished. As he slowly made his way out with the crowd, he overheard two Dublin working men going over the argument with analytical perception. He realised that Hammond understood his audience!

Occasionally notable Roman Catholic speakers would come to Dublin to give a lecture in one of the public halls or theatres. One of the senior workers would attend, take notes, and then go back to the Mission to report. Over tea-time Hammond would work on updating a reply (he would already have his basic message prepared) while sandwich board men went up and down the streets proclaiming, 'Father A— will be answered to-night in the Mission building, Townsend Street'. And so it would be.

One of the best known of these occasions was when Hammond responded to a lecture given by Monsignor Ronald Knox (translator of the Knox Version). After a somewhat sheltered upbringing as an Anglican, Knox had become a Roman Catholic. His lecture was entitled 'The Wane of Protestantism'. Hammond took as the text for his reply: 'He feedeth on ashes, a deluded mind has lead him astray' (*Isa.* 44:20). Knox's father, by contrast, was an evangelical Church of England bishop, and had written the preface to Hammond's booklet *Does the Doctrine of*

Transubstantiation Involve a Material Change?

Tom Murray served as Hammond's right hand man. The two were complete opposites: Hammond from Cork was warm, humorous and well-fed looking; Murray was northern, serious, very conservative, thin shouldered and spoke through his nose. But they worked in perfect tandem. Murray was nicknamed 'Oul Search d'Scriptures' and overcame all obstacles by loving persistence. Often he went visiting with his own food in his pocket to give to those he knew had nothing in the house to eat. He was attacked on a number of occasions, once with a knife, to which he said he could not retaliate since his assailant was a lady! He had a deep knowledge of the Roman Controversy and kept a carefully annotated, interleaved, copy of Blakeney's *Manual* on the Controversy with him. Years later, when Hammond was leaving Ireland for the last time (after a return visit home in 1947-48) and was being escorted by a young worker to the North Wall to get the boat to England his parting words were 'Pick Tom Murray's brains'.[4]

Another worker and close family friend whose name is everywhere linked with the work was Monica Farrell. Brought up in a Roman Catholic family, three of her sisters were nuns, a brother a priest and another a monk. She had argued vigorously for her Catholic faith at school, but the quiet ways of a Presbyterian school friend, who had in her Bible the answers that Monica could never find, convinced her that her Church was wrong. When she left the Roman Catholic Church she really believed that Martin Luther was the last person to have left it. This was the start of a life in the service of biblical truth carried on in Ireland and later in Australia.

Since the number of Mission staff approached a hundred

in those days it is not possible even to name them all; but under Hammond, whether they worked in the Laundry, taught in the Schools, engaged in visiting or kept accounts, they worked loyally and hard. They met in the mornings for prayer and spent a conference week together in the autumn when a visiting speaker would give devotional addresses. The younger workers, still in training, were lectured in the mornings by the senior staff, during which many a yawn was stifled as Hammond expanded on Salmon's *Infallibility of the Church*.

Normally Hammond did not interfere in what the staff did; he was busy, as they were. However one occasion is remembered as having been important enough for him to call all the workers together. They attended worship in the Mission Church on Sundays, but outside of that were free to go to other churches and meetings. However Hammond had heard that some were regularly going to a Baptist Church and beginning to be unsettled by the zeal with which Baptists were promoting their views. Everybody was assembled and Hammond spelt out at length the paedobaptist position. For most of the workers that was the end of the matter, though one worker later became a Baptist pastor in Northern Ireland. All who are involved in Christian ministry will appreciate another piece of advice he gave his workers: 'Get a sense of humour or get out of Christian work; without a sense of humour it will be the death of you'.[5]

HARD WORK
Hammond had a heavy administrative work load of 'cases'. He followed up and answered many matters in the newspapers. When an evangelist working in a County Mayo town

had his books 'confiscated' and was chased out of town, Hammond took the matter up and wrote demanding their return. In those days when feelings ran high questions such as who had buried a workhouse convert, or who had taken care of or baptized a particular orphan (known by lawyers as *Habeas Animam* cases) occupied columns of newsprint. The Roman Catholic Church, with huge orphanages of its own and control of most hospices and homes, was prepared to spare no effort in tracking down anyone who left its fold to become a member of any other, whether they were alive or dead.

To trumped-up charges of malpractice Hammond wisely replied by asking for specific evidence. On eleven occasions he went to law on behalf of individual Protestants or converts who had been deprived of their rights. He won ten of the cases and in the other the party spirited herself 'outside of the Court's jurisdiction' and, since there had already been much publicity the matter was not followed up. In such cases, unpopular and unprofitable for professional lawyers, Hammond had to become his own lawyer and find out how the law could protect his clients. The bulk of his 'case-work' came through mixed marriages. The *Ne Temere* decree promulgated by Pius X came into force in 1908 and made binding for Roman Catholics what had only been a matter of *de facto* practice: before any Protestant could be married to a Roman Catholic in a Roman Catholic service—and no other form of marriage was approved—the Protestant had to sign away all rights to bring up any children in the Protestant faith.

This church legislation virtually assumed the standing of civil law and on occasion was supported by the Courts. It was forced on young people at a time when they were emotionally very vulnerable. Although the law has been modified, it is still in force. Throughout his years in the Mission Hammond dealt with a constant stream of clergymen, mostly in the Church of Ireland, who had to deal with sad and difficult cases of mixed marriages.

Despite his busy schedule, Hammond made time to travel throughout Ireland and his visits brought encouragement to many. Wicklow was a favourite place. When there he stayed with Dr Synge, Rector of Derralossory, a missionary home from China and the father of J. M. Synge the playwright. There he got to know the Horan family, one of whose sons, Tom, later served as his curate and became Superintendent of the Mission.

Even outside Dublin his reputation made him a target for vituperation and mob-violence. As late as 1933, when speaking in North Strand Church, Dublin, he recounted a visit to Limerick: 'I was in Limerick on Thursday. I was escorted from the train to the YMCA by Civic Guards, and back again.'[6] This was not surprising for Limerick had the reputation of being an exceptionally difficult area for evangelism. While conducting a medical mission, both Dr Long and his patients were frequently abused. The doctor had been boycotted, and a cabman even took his horse out of the shafts of his side-car rather than drive him.[7]

Each year Hammond took deputation meetings for the ICM, speaking at centres throughout England, but it is not possible to say to what extent his listeners came to hear him out of concern for the Irish rather than because he had the name of being 'a good Protestant'. It is possible that a very Protestant faction in the English Church saw him as a stick with which to beat the Ritualists.

He also travelled in England working with students and

leading evangelistic missions. As one of the early stalwarts in the spread of the Inter-Varsity Fellowship in the late 1920s he was added to its advisory committee where he served with other leading evangelical figures.

Prayer Book revision was in the air at this time, and changes were being talked about which would introduce doctrinal error to Anglicanism. Again Hammond's assistance was valued. This took him on a lecture tour of Canada and Australia in 1926, of which we shall hear more later.

The Hammond family was now growing up. They had moved to Dartry Road in 1929. The boys had gone through the motor-bike phase and were leaving home. John, the eldest, had been away from home, in effect, since childhood. Thomas ('Chat'), a brilliant student, was, at that stage, an evangelical. He left in 1932 and became for a while a tutor at the London College of Divinity before becoming a vicar of noted High Churchmanship in England. John and he married two sisters. Carl, quieter and more studious, left home shortly afterwards, and was ordained in the Church of Ireland. He served as a curate in Willowfield, Belfast before following his father to Australia where he worked widely in Victoria and New South Wales. He taught briefly at Moore College and remained an evangelical. Doris went to Trinity College like her father and older brothers and eventually travelled with her parents to Australia.

THE HOMES
But T. C. Hammond had another and bigger family. He involved himself deeply with the children of the Homes connected with the Mission. Each child had a story of neglect, bereavement or virtual abandonment. The Homes,

institutional and spartan as they may have been, were for most of the children the only home they knew in childhood. From there they went out into life to make the best they could of themselves. Some never overcame their poor start in life. Most found quiet everyday niches in society for themselves. A handful distinguished themselves in Christian service. One boy from the Homes, Albert Shaw, was for many years the hard working head of the Dublin Christian Mission.

Hammond came to see the children often and even took some of them with him on his travels to England. But the best event for them all was the annual holiday. The children from the country Homes would come up to the city, and down to lovely County Wicklow, with its soft hills and granite walls, would go the city children. The train brought them as far as Aughrim; the older ones would then walk while the small ones and the luggage would be carried the remaining miles to the Home at Sheanagh by farm cart loaned for the day by a local grocer.

The oversight of the Homes had been inherited when Hammond came to the Mission in 1919, but he saw a very human need that was not being met by any of them. So in 1921 in the face of opposition, even from friends, he pushed through the establishment of 'The Children's Fold'. It was to be for illegitimate children. Four hundred and sixty-one children had been admitted by the time he left in 1936. The Report of the Fold for that year says:

Many phases of Mr Hammond's work have earned undying fame, but none is more worthy of commendation than this one in which he has made possible, in some measure, the fulfilment of our Lord's command, 'Suffer the little children to come unto Me.'

YMCA group in Cork (c.1895)
Back Row: centre, George Bird; extreme left, G.R. Harding Wood
Centre row: centre, John McNay; on his right, T.C. Hammond

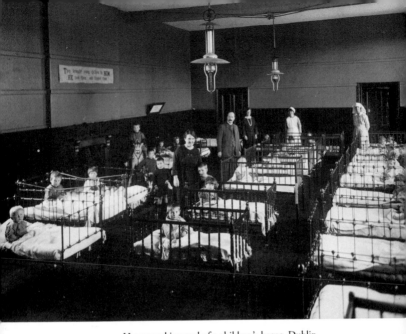

Hammond in ward of a children's home, Dublin

Hammond, seated, centre right, with Mission workers in Dublin (c.1935)

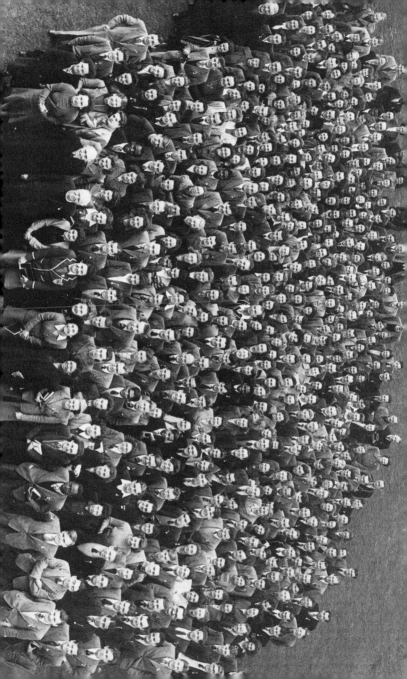

Hammond when Principal of Moore Theological College, Sydney

The same Report describes it as an essential aspect of 'Protestant' work in Dublin. But those who saw Hammond's eyes fill with tears as he appealed for the children knew that his motives were purer than partisanship.

THE PRAYER BOOK VISIT TO AUSTRALIA

Not even this heavy workload exhausted Hammond's activities in the inter-war years. As the Incumbent of the Mission Church—a status he had to extract from the Diocesan authorities—he also had the normal pastoral duties of a church to attend to. In addition he was a popular speaker at lunch time meetings organised by evangelical students in 'Number 40' of Trinity College. The numbers were small but they were keen and his teaching was sound and practical. Among his listeners were many future clergymen, including a Dean, and a young medical student, Denis Burkitt, who later became famous as the 'Fibre Doctor' and contributed in a major way to a revolution in western eating patterns.

Hammond also spoke at the meetings of the College Theological Society, which were 'frock coat' occasions. Here he held his own against men like Charles Osborne a leading Anglo-Catholic, H. D. A. Major a Modernist and A. Arthur Robinson, the brother of Armitage Robinson and father of John, later Bishop of Woolwich of *Honest to God* fame. Hammond gave his support to the Bible Churchmen's Missionary Society (BCMS) when it was formed because of a falling away from biblical theology among some leaders in the Church Missionary Society. He was one of the earliest BCMS speakers in Ireland. He went on a number of occasions to Keswick to represent the ICM, and, when there, he was put in charge of the open-air meetings.

On one occasion in Dublin in the early 1920s a committee invited the American evangelist and teacher R. A. Torrey to give a series of lectures in the Rotunda Room. On the day they were to commence Torrey's ship was delayed in docking at Cobh. With only hours in hand they approached Hammond, and he took the opening meetings—so well, apparently, that they asked themselves 'Why did we look elsewhere for a speaker when we had such an evangelist on the doorstep?' When the Mission did get under way Torrey called in Hammond to deal with something he had never encountered before. He had his trained counsellors for their work in the 'enquiry room' but when he met with the 'Thou art Peter, and on this rock I will build my church' syndrome the call went out, 'Mr Hammond, Mr Hammond, there's someone here wants to talk with you!'[8]

The Presbyterian evangelist W. P. Nicholson was also at the height of his energies about the same time. Hundreds of working people in Belfast had made professions of faith through his ministry. He had a reputation for blunt and at times crude language. When he came to Dublin to speak in 1925 this side of his ministry was attacked by those who did not like his work. Hammond spoke up in his defence: 'Those who criticise Nicholson know little of how working men communicate. Do they suppose the truths of Christianity always require genteel drawing room talk?'[9]

Hammond was always a welcome return visitor to St Kevin's; in 1930 he spoke at the Dedication of their War Memorial when nine hundred and fifty people were present. Whether on the city pavements or in arenas of intellectual debate he was always able to commend his

Lord, effectively, lovingly, and appropriately to the occasion. He was versatile and had a great warmth of affection for people.

An opponent of Roman Catholicism, Hammond was also against its Anglican manifestation which had surfaced as Tractarianism under J. H. Newman and W. Froude in the early nineteenth century and by the addition of ritualism had developed into Anglo-Catholicism. In England there was considerable pressure to revise the Prayer Book in order to subvert doctrine and to introduce advanced 'catholic' practices. This came to a head in the narrowly defeated 1928 attempt to introduce a revised Prayer Book.

Evangelical Anglicans throughout the world were alarmed and an invitation came to Hammond to give a series of lectures, financed by the Vickery Trust. He responded in keeping with his inability to say 'No' and travelled on his own via Canada giving lectures in Toronto, Winnipeg and Vancouver, and then on to Australia, speaking in every state except Queensland. While in Sydney he came to the notice of H. L. Tress, one of the trustees of Moore College. He was away for nearly a year and on his return he was given an illuminated address from the workers in the Mission. They did not want to lose him and they wanted him to know that they were very glad to see him return.

Quietly and with a confidentiality that robbed him of the credit, Hammond came to the help of leaders of the Church of Ireland as, for example, when Archbishop Gregg, grandson of Bishop Gregg of Cork, but not a man of the same convictions, became involved in a dispute with Cardinal MacRory over the validity of 'non-Catholic' ministers.

This debate was conducted in the pages of the *Irish Times* in 1931. MacRory had asserted that the Protestant church had no part or place in the Church of Christ. It was known that Gregg came to Hammond for help. Allegedly Hammond said, in as many words, 'If you had come to me in the first place you would not have got yourself into the position you are in now'! The debate continued, and then suddenly MacRory stopped. It is alleged that he was told to stop because 'they know too much'.

Hammond later clashed with the same Cardinal in 1935 over the use by Protestant colporteurs of the Coyne edition of the Douay Scriptures (published by Coyne without notes but with an *imprimatur*).

Archbishop Gregg also came to Hammond on other matters, one being to ask him to use his influence on the YMCA to see that the Church of Ireland was given better representation in its affairs. To many clergy Hammond was unacceptable, and being connected with the ICM was a stigma, but as Dr A. A. Luce of Trinity College once said, 'They don't want to be identified with Hammond, but when things get rough they are prepared to shelter behind his guns'.[10]

The 1930s were dull years in Ireland; in both North and South the Governments were restrictive, generally negative and sectarian. The Unionist Party in the North was striving to maintain a 'Protestant Parliament for a Protestant people', but effectively to the detriment of both. The South was a grey and joyless Free State as the economic war with England brought the country almost to bankruptcy.

The Roman Catholic Church was firmly in the saddle. A rigid but ludicrous censorship was in force. Religion was occupied with the trivia of legalism. A church paper,

The Standard (January 1930), seriously answered questions about whether Irish people could start their Friday fast by 'sun' time, which in Ireland is twenty to twenty-five minutes later than 'clock' time. The answer was 'Yes'. There was also an extraordinary debate over whether one could fulfil the obligation to attend mass while standing outside the chapel door. The 'maximum observance' rule demanded attendance properly in the pew with full attention and participation. However if the main church door is open, one is part of the congregation; if it is closed one is excluded. But what about the inner door of the church? Since this door's function is merely to exclude draughts it cannot be regarded as a 'door of exclusion'; therefore one can fulfil obligation while remaining outside a closed inner door, and many did. Legalism had its Protestant manifestations too. Much that passed for religion in the North was largely an expression of the fallacious assumption, 'I don't drink, smoke, or read Sunday papers, therefore I'm a Christian'.

Throughout the countryside many of the former 'Big Houses' which had escaped being burned to the ground in the Troubles, had become Monasteries and Convents. In 1932 Dublin was host to a Eucharistic Congress. This gave concrete expression to the notion that to be Irish was to be Catholic. Government ministers were to the fore in giving homage to church dignitaries; the famous Irish tenor, 'Count' John McCormack sang hymns to the crowds. Townsend Street carried a banner 'Long live the Trinity' aimed at the Mission as if it were a cult, and Church of Ireland churches in the city were expected not to ring their bells on the Sunday. Even so, during the Congress one or two brave men attempted open-airs. The Congress was a powerful demonstration, but it was also the high water mark of Irish Catholicism, for external and internal forces which would challenge the Church's hegemony were already at work.

Yet, in this inhospitable climate Hammond and his team were reaping a spiritual harvest. During his time as Superintendent over five hundred people openly professed conversion. These converts well illustrated the apostolic observation that not many wise, powerful or of noble birth are called into Christ's kingdom (*1 Cor.* 1:26). Humanly speaking this would seem to be one of the reasons why, despite much effort, little lasting impact was made on the religious life of Dublin society. Little conscious attempt was made to influence the more 'influential' groups in the life of the city.

Each person signed a register in the Mission declaring that he or she was acting freely and out of personal conviction, and each signature was witnessed by two people. Such a safeguard was needed since the Mission was always open to hostile criticism and charges of fraudulent proselytising. Sometimes it was necessary to see that new converts had an escort in case they were spirited away. Most were received into the Church of Ireland, but where clergy and bishops belonged to the world of golf and cricket clubs, cathedrals and freemasonry, little genuine spiritual help was available. The subsequent histories of these 'converts' are mixed. Some were forced to leave home; more chose to do so. Some fitted into the life of other city churches; others slipped back into old ways. A few went on to fruitful Christian service of one sort or another.

In a special category of converts were a number of priests who left the Church of Rome. These included Father

Aldama who had first turned to Anglo-Catholicism but found it too similar to what he had left. Among other converted priests were Father Casella, who after being received into the Church of Ireland was a curate on the Shankill Road in Belfast for a while; Father Flores who eventually went to Sydney Diocese; Father Verri who became a Methodist minister in his native Italy and Brother Plankeart who worked as a colporteur before going to Canada. There were about twenty in all. Some of these former priests lived in the Mission House for their own safety, receiving instruction from Hammond, for several months.

Of special interest is Hammond's first interview with Father Flores who was from Malta and had been a missionary in Mesopotamia. Flores and his party had been attacked in the desert by tribesmen. He had dug down into the sand and had said an act of contrition to make his peace with God. However, he survived, and it occurred to him that had he been killed he would have been right with God, but now he would have to go to confession before a priest. This led him to question the basis of his faith. In the interview Hammond began by explaining the gospel grounds for forgiveness of sins. Flores merely smiled a little disdainfully, so Hammond stopped and said:

I know you're thinking that you've heard it all before and it's just what you'd expect me to say. Well, let me tell you what you believe. You believe that your sins were washed away in baptism, the virtues of faith, hope and charity were infused, and that you were alright until you ran into mortal sin. Then you had to avail yourself of the second plank after shipwreck and make confession to a priest, with due dispositions. Eternal punishment was then removed, but you still had to meet the temporal punishment by almsgiving, fasting and austerities here and purgatory hereafter.

Flores listened after that.[11]

THE CALL OF SYDNEY

In late 1935 the Australian visit of nine years earlier had its reverberations when the key position of Principal of Moore College, Sydney, became vacant. The trustees invited Hammond to take the post and to serve simultaneously as rector of St Philip's Church in the city. He was by now approaching sixty years of age.

Hammond appreciated the importance of the job to which he was called, and the strategic importance of Moore College, and it is possible that after years in the negative world of controversy the more positive work of teaching was appealing. He also was encouraged by his wife's views. The transition took place quite quickly. There was a round of farewell visits, including Belfast and among his longest-standing friends in Cork.

Just at that time, however, Hammond had agreed to write a book of basic doctrine for the Inter-Varsity Fellowship. This was at the request of the London Inter-Faculty Christian Union who had held a special mission to the whole University of London entitled 'Out of World Chaos'. That they should have asked Hammond, an Irishman, indicates the paucity of evangelical scholars at that time. Something not too technical was wanted to help students who had recently come to faith in Christ. Christian publishing at that stage was somewhat old-fashioned, heroic and too pietistic in its ethos to be able to provide solid foundational teaching for these young men and women.

Douglas Johnson, the great driving force in Inter-Varsity in its early days, was asked to interview Hammond to see if

he were 'sound'. Johnson also gave an outline of the areas
that should be covered in the proposed book. He reported
back to the committee that they themselves could go next
time for obviously from what he had heard they were all
only ninety per cent sound!

Hammond said he would need help in order to get the
manuscript finished before he emigrated, so Johnson, the
nameless 'young graduate' mentioned in the Preface of the
book, came over and acted as his assistant. (Johnson was, in
fact, thirty-one at the time!).

Both men worked long hours into the night. Douglas
Johnson said afterwards that he saw scarcely anything of
Dublin except the road from the boat to the Mission and
back.[12] They finished it, and Hammond corrected the
proofs on the ship to Australia. That was how his best
known work, *In Understanding Be Men,* came to be written, and perhaps explains its being 'a very rapid survey'.[13]

The staff of the Mission and other friends had a magnificent farewell meeting for him in Dublin on 20 February
1936. Archbishop Gregg was in the chair. He spoke well,
albeit in a diplomatic way, of Hammond: 'We are losing
one who has served the Church of Ireland for a long time.
He has served it very faithfully and very consistently.'[14]

Hammond was then presented with a silver tray
ornamented with a Celtic design from the Book of Kells
and inscribed 'From the Archbishops, Bishops and other
friends, Clerical and Lay as a token of esteem.' He replied
by saying: 'I have always loved the Church of Ireland, I was
born in it, baptised in it, confirmed and ordained in it'. He
spoke of his controversial work among Catholics by saying
it had been done 'not for any feeling of animosity, but
because we yearn over them and have such a high opinion

of them.' But there was a strong feeling among Church of Ireland people and others in Dublin that rather than let Hammond go, the Church should have appointed him as a bishop or, perhaps more appropriately, taking a cue from the Australians, given him a professorship in the Divinity School.

Hammond's successor as rector of St Kevin's, Richard Bird, voiced these thoughts when he spoke: 'We are sorry that the honour which we feel should have come from our own Church should come from another Continent.' But lest anyone should have thought that Hammond was leaving out of umbrage, another friend and evangelical clergyman, N. D. Emerson said: 'He is not going because he didn't get preferment, God has called him and for no other reason . . . I do believe that the Church of Ireland won't experience a bigger loss in your day or mine.'

Privately Hammond made the point that it is necessary to leave to be appreciated, and many felt it was easy for the bishops to show their esteem when he was leaving. *The Irish Catholic* (not to be confused with *The Catholic*, which Hammond edited) poured out pent-up venom after he left, and in doing so made public the widely-felt hostility to evangelical Protestantism:

We cannot congratulate Australian Protestants on their acquisition . . .the notorious chief of Soupers . . . he stage managed a notorious renegade Catholic named Monica Farrell in order to blackguard Catholic priests and nuns . . . He will carry with him the curses of many a drunken mother and father whose children's souls were lost through the devilish work of the spiritual harpies of whom Rev Hammond was chief.

A barren tree does not have sticks thrown at it! The

Mission held a special meeting to refute these charges. The pertinent question was then asked:' Why did they wait until he was gone to say such things?'

The Mission staff and the Irish Committee gave Hammond a silver plate for a roll-top desk to be bought in Sydney. In fact a radiogram was bought instead. They accompanied him, his wife and daughter, Doris, to the boat-train at Westland Row, (now Pearse Station), for a tearful farewell.

Ireland had lost a true patriot. Padraic Pearse, the 1916 leader had claimed that an unfree Ireland would never be at peace, but Hammond knew that spiritual freedom was more profound than any political freedom. Only as the Son of God sets men free from sin are they free indeed (*John* 8:34-36).

6

'To Australia's Sunny Shore . . .'

I n March 1936, following their personal and public
farewells in Ireland and England the Hammonds—
'TC', his wife Margaret (or 'Gert' as he called her) and
their daughter—sailed for Australia on the Orient liner
Orford. Archbishop Mowll had made the same journey on
the same ship two years before them. It was to become an
early loss in the Second World War, being bombed and
sunk at Marseilles in 1940.

The undisturbed time afforded by the month-long
relaxed voyage to Australia was used by Hammond to read
and correct the proofs of *In Understanding Be Men,* often
sweating over them in the tropics. He wrote in his author's
Preface that he 'strove to complete the volume amid the
rush of meetings and the upheavals consequent upon the
transfer of his home to Sydney.' Hence, 'He would ask for
indulgence from his theological brethren for any technical
errors that may have escaped his scrutiny.'

The Hammonds arrived on 14 April. Archbishop Mowll
was anxious to get things moving and had arranged a gruel-
ling first day for his new man. The students of Moore
College were called at half-past four that morning to be
ready to welcome him, long before the *Orford* had entered

the Heads of Sydney Harbour. As the liner made its stately way up the harbour a large and inquisitive, if also mildly apprehensive, reception party was assembling. So much was at stake; so much was hanging on one man's suitability for the job. No one at the quayside had any doubt that a new page had been turned in the life of the Church in Australia and the first words of a new chapter were just about to be written.

The press came aboard and the new Principal was photographed and interviewed, *The Daily Telegraph* [Sydney] had already carried his photograph captioned 'Noted Theologist arrives'. Instead of looking his age (now nearly sixty) he seemed to many to be only about forty-five. He was taken to the College for a welcome at half-past ten. In the afternoon he met diocesan clergy in the Chapter House and was instituted as Rector of St Philip's that same evening. The Archbishop preached on the St Kevin's text: 'Sirs, we would see Jesus'. Friend, foe and fence-sitter were given early opportunity to meet him.

THE DIOCESE OF SYDNEY

That there should have been such interest in Hammond's new appointment was due more to the previous history and peculiar situation of the Diocese of Sydney than it was to Hammond himself.[1]

The Diocese of Sydney is known throughout the Anglican Church world-wide as being strongly evangelical. It represents the church of the Thirty-Nine Articles, the Book of Common Prayer, the biblical convictions of Cranmer, Hooker, Jewel, Ussher, Whitefield and J. C. Ryle. It symbolises for many the Anglicanism that is still concerned with evangelism and the trustworthiness of the Bible.

On that Australian autumn day Hammond arrived to take up the second most responsible position in a diocese which, as such, had been in existence for less than ninety years. The origins of the church in Sydney did, however, go back further, to 1788 when Richard Johnson, a Church of England clergyman arrived with the First Fleet as its chaplain. Johnson was an evangelical as were most of the early clergy. There had also been a strong Irish input from the outset including the colourful Henry Fulton a Church of Ireland clergyman who landed in Sydney in 1800—as a convict. He had been implicated in a minor way in the 1798 Rebellion led by Wolf Tone and inspired by the French Revolution. However, because of the great shortage of clergy Fulton was quickly rehabilitated and served long and well.

The Irish and the Australians share in having a major English involvement in their history. They also share a whimsical view of English formality. Many Irish clergy were attracted to Australia as a less claustrophobic sphere of work than ministering at home to an inward-looking minority, for the most part made up of landlords and their servants. With the need to provide clergy for such a vast continent Irish ministers were always welcomed in Australia. Hammond, for example, was to be the fourth Irish rector of St Philip's, and throughout the 1930s and 1940s would be one of a strong 'Irish connection' with considerable influence in the Diocese.

BROUGHTON, BARKER, BARRY

The pioneering years passed and the colony grew beyond its convict roots. In due course Australia itself became a diocese, having previously been under the direction of the Bishop of Calcutta. In June 1836 William Grant Broughton, a high churchman of the old school was made Bishop and installed in St James' Church, Sydney. His sermon on that occasion was on justification by faith.

Church life was not easy, complex issues had to be dealt with at an enormous distance from England. Diocesan machinery had to be put in place. The populace were not church minded. This was hardly surprising since they had been largely English criminals or Irish rebels. In addition, many of the free settlers had come to Australia to get 'away from all that religion'. It has been said that whereas America had been colonised by the Pilgrim Fathers, Australia was colonised by the 'Prodigal Sons'!

During his episcopate (1836-53), Broughton had kept a firm hand on the diocese. While not himself an evangelical (he was tolerant of tractarianism) he had maintained conditions under which the already existing evangelical nature of Sydney churchmanship could grow. He died in 1853 and was followed by Frederick Barker (1855-82) an earnest and clear evangelical. He had served in Ireland and Liverpool and took a firm line against Roman Catholicism, as well as opposing incipient Anglo-Catholicism within Anglicanism.

The colony was now moving slowly away from Mother England and recognising the need for Australian men in the ministry. Barker was largely instrumental in setting up Moore College,[2] following on the vision and efforts of Broughton and using the financial help of Thomas Moore a carpenter and early settler.

Barker was succeeded by Alfred Barry (1884-89) of King's College, London. It would be another eighty years before the diocese would be headed by an Australian, in the person of Marcus Loane (1966-82). Barry was the first bishop to be elected, the previous men being crown appointments. Even so the election was manipulated and controversial. Barry was 'low' in churchmanship and made considerable contributions in the area of education, but he was not decidedly evangelical. If anything, the fact that he was not 'one of them' united the evangelicals. During his comparatively short term of office two events galvanised evangelicals into a coherent force.

Albeit in good faith, Barry had made an unfortunate appointment to Moore College. Assuming him to be a moderate churchman he had installed Thomas Hill as Principal. In fact Hill turned out to be a tractarian in both teaching and practice and eventually was, in effect, dismissed.

The second matter concerned an ornamental reredos in the Cathedral, one panel of which depicted the crucifixion. Strong objections were voiced and, with the Anglican genius for compromise it was replaced by a transfiguration scene. Evangelicals were now more concerned than ever to guard what they had.

The next election was again an unfortunate and pro-tracted business. During the confusion the saintly Handley Moule (subsequently bishop of Durham) was elected but declined. After subsequent chess-like moves William Saumarez Smith (1890-1909) of St. Aidan's College, Birkenhead was appointed. He was clearly an evangelical and gave leadership as the battle with growing secularism became increasingly urgent.

Smith served during the last decade of the nineteenth century and the first decade of the twentieth. It was a rap-idly changing world, churchmen were no longer respected leaders in society or unchallenged in their basic teaching.

The theories and teaching of Darwinism, secularism and modernism were no longer confined to rarefied intellectual studies; they were becoming the possession of everyman, and were popular because they agreed so well with the humanism of unregenerate man. Bishop (after 1897, Archbishop) Smith quietly encouraged his diocese to grow out to the people and his calm control allowed others to develop ministries.

Under Smith's leadership missions of far-reaching consequence were held. George Grubb, a Church of Ireland clergyman came to Australia and New Zealand. His preaching echoed the 'Keswick' message of consecration and in a series of missions gave new impetus to the arid evangelicalism of some, while he challenged others with the need for evangelism and missionary work. His work coalesced with that of another Irishman, Mervyn Archdall, Rector of Balmain. (Coincidentally it was the same Tipperary-born Archdall who baptized T. C. Hammond in Cork.) Another significant figure in this movement was Nathaniel Jones, principal of Moore College (1897-1911).

Future leaders of the church in Sydney were converted at this time; many were motivated to go to overseas mission fields; personal holiness was encouraged and prayer unions started. Evangelicalism in Sydney as well as in Melbourne and other parts of Australia received a powerful stimulus. But there was also a debit side: the emphasis was moved from the objectivity of the atonement to the subjectivity of the believer's own experience. The teaching was introspective at the personal level, separatist at society level and speculative in its interests in the last things. Christians were given excessive encouragement either to look in to themselves or away to the (imminent) return of Christ. By doing so they in effect opted out of society and failed to be the salt of the earth.

J. C. WRIGHT

When Archbishop Smith died in 1909 he left a stronger, more confident diocese, and also one in which Synod had more control. His successor, John Charles Wright (1909-1933) was Archdeacon of Manchester, to which office he had been appointed by E. A. Knox, at that time England's most outstanding evangelical bishop. Wright was a rising evangelical, yet a moderate in churchmanship and determined to be scrupulously fair. His fairness was quickly to be tested.

Since 1900 the clergy of St James', the fashionable and influential city church, had been using the chasuble, a large round garment without seams regarded by its wearers and opponents alike as the quintessential 'priestly' vestment. Because of its history and associations its use was not merely a matter of ecclesiastical fashion but a powerful Anglo-Catholic symbol. The parish of St James was vacant when Wright was installed as Archbishop, but some months later an appointment was made. Wright stepped in by refusing to appoint the nominee, Dean Kite of Hobart, unless he undertook not to wear the chasuble. Kite refused and declined the post.

Criticism was heaped on the Archbishop. Perhaps the most hurtful being that he was only acting at the behest of his evangelical handlers. But he held his ground and courteously went to a service in a packed church to explain his position. He insisted that he did not intend to change the churchmanship of St James, but would not allow illegal vestments. When angry Anglo-Catholics brought pressure to bear on possible replacement appointees the Archbishop said he would be left with no option but to appoint an evangelical. In the face of such a 'threat' the Anglo-Catholics relented and a compromise candidate was appointed. This stand served Wright well. A couple of years later a vacancy occurred in the ritualist Christ Church St Laurence in Pitt St. The incoming rector had to dispense with the chasuble which had been in use for years. (It is of more than antiquarian significance that the actual garment is now on display in a glass case in the church.)

Archbishop Wright held office for nearly a quarter of a century. During that time the diocese went through the terrible Australian coming of age: the First World War. The country lost proportionately more men than any other combatant nation, yet it saw explosive suburban growth and accelerated church building. It also suffered through the depression of the 1930s which hit Australia, a primary producer, especially hard. Meantime, however, as the threat of ritualism was contained, the sharp edge of evangelicalism seemed to be blunted, and more men identified with what became known as Liberal Evangelicalism.

Wright had not enjoyed good health in the latter half of his episcopate, and this, coupled with his irenical running of diocesan affairs, meant that he did not provide the leadership for which evangelicals looked. They were determined that his successor would be more distinctly evangelical and a more definite leader.

MOWLL

In Howard Mowll (1934-58), ex-President of Cambridge Inter-Collegiate Christian Union (CICCU), Bishop of West China, evangelicals were given the man they were looking for.

Dean Talbot and Archdeacon Davies, Principal of Moore College, the leading liberal evangelicals in the diocese had put forward Joseph Hunkin of Rugby. Hunkin had an evangelical understanding of grace, but his scholarship had been influenced by liberalism. When his candidacy was discussed he was soon labelled as a 'modernist' largely on account of the company with which he was associated. He was rejected and Mowll was appointed.

Mowll was single-minded in his vision, but unfamiliar with the church politics of a large diocese. His great enthusiasm brought strong and definite, if not always wise, leadership but his evangelical credentials were beyond reproach. Elected in 1933 he came to Sydney and took up office in March 1934. When Hammond was appointed, he was still himself something of a 'new boy' at the head of a dynamic but somewhat restless diocese. Both clergy and people, always intensely watchful of their Archbishop's leadership, were reading every sign they could in his decisions to try to discern which way the ball would bounce.

As the new Principal of Moore College, Hammond was bound to play an influential role in the diocese, and that is why his arrival and first moves were keenly watched. *The Outlook*, a small paper with a private circulation among some of the Sydney clergy, had already entered the fray. It expressed concern that 'his appointment will not heal the breaches . . . we have no need for the religious enmities of the Old World.' It poured scorn on the claim that he was 'the best available': he was middle-aged; he belonged to the Church of Ireland and so was not from the centre of Anglican life; he had worked in an atmosphere of controversy.

This critique was sustained, and the March 1936 issue

asserted that, 'unless he is less intractable than on his former visit his success will only come through the withdrawal of many liberal minded men from all matters outside their own parishes'—words which said more about the lack of an open spirit among liberals than they did about Hammond. Even Mowll, who had not met him before making the appointment, watched and listened anxiously at first lest Hammond should prove to be the extremist some feared.

Little of this bothered Hammond himself. He had come in the full maturity of his teaching powers, convinced of God's call and the importance of the job before him. His only concession to the watchfulness of the diocese and the college was an almost mischievous determination to show them what an Irishman could do. He made his mark very quickly. One of his first lectures at Moore College—on the transcendence of God—was so demanding intellectually that it left the students reeling. Wrote one observer, euphemistically: 'he has a distinctly philosophical approach not always appreciated by those unacquainted with the rules of the syllogism.'[3]

The new Principal lectured on most subjects in the College curriculum, including the Old and New Testament, the Prayer Book, and Philosophy of Religion (for which he was also a lecturer in Sydney University and an examiner in the Australian College of Theology). But he is best remembered for his teaching in Dogmatics, in which he used Griffith Thomas' *The Principles of Theology* as the basic textbook with occasional references to his own *In Understanding Be Men.*

He was soon active on the floor of Synod, speaking on Sydney's perennial subject, the Constitution. His maiden speech was in reply to one by Dr P. H. Micklem, rector of

St James (whose commentary on the Gospel of Matthew was published in the Westminster Commentary Series). Hammond started with an Irish story which broke the tension and then proceeded to demolish Micklem's polished argument piece by piece.

On his feet at Synod, Hammond demonstrated his remarkable powers of recall for facts and references. He was always at his best when his back was against the wall. He fought hard, but always on principles—he could never understand why some opponents took his remarks personally. Some called him arrogant, others said he was 'an evil genius' and used the old slur, accusing him of 'not really being an Anglican'.

At that time he had a famous namesake in the Diocese, Archdeacon R. B. S. Hammond. Even the press sometimes assumed that they were brothers. R. B. S. Hammond, a rugged individualist, strongly averse to committee activity, had done magnificent work in evangelism and social welfare, even founding a pioneering relief community which later became the Sydney suburb of Hammondville. Soon the two Hammonds were close friends, on the strength of which 'RBS' told 'TC' to tone down his Irish jokes if he wanted to be taken seriously! Hammond did tend to trade on the fool's pardon that was extended to his Irish impishness.

Shortly after his arrival the diocese celebrated the Centennial of Bishop Broughton. 'TC' was asked to propose the vote of thanks in the Great Hall of Sydney University in reply to a speech by Archbishop D'Arcy of Armagh, a visitor for the celebrations. He appreciated the honour and as the subject matter was philosophical, the Idealism of Berkeley, he was in his element. He also played the part of

Archbishop Saumerez Smith in a pageant for the Deaconess Institution. Thus in a very short time he made his mark on diocesan activities. He had also written his longest book, *Perfect Freedom*, within a year of his arrival.

Soon Hammond was joined by his son Carl who had been a curate in Willowfield, Belfast, and by Carl's fiancee, Gwen, from Portarlington in County Laois whom he had not met before. Carl along with other young clergy had come to Australia in response to a call from Mowll.

MOWLL AND 'TC'.

Hammond's relationship with the Archbishop also strengthened his place in diocesan life. Mowll needed Hammond; Mowll had the heart, the energy, the flair for the work, but he lacked theological depth, and needed a deep thinker as a resource person. And so during their long working partnership—they were almost exact contemporaries in Sydney (Mowll 1934-58, Hammond 1936-61)—they complemented one another. The Archbishop often sought the advice of his college Principal, and it was well understood in Sydney that some of Mowll's most important speeches and decisions were in fact Hammond's.

It is probably true that Hammond also needed Mowll. He certainly needed the freedom and scope which Mowll allowed him. He had never had this with the Irish bishops who had only grudgingly given him respect. Hammond soon became an establishment figure, a force in the diocese, and one of the small group who held most of the power in church affairs. This was very different from his position in Dublin where he had always been an outsider in the corridors of power.

In this context it is interesting to compare the Dublin

Hammond with the Sydney Hammond. The comparison is like that of a politician who after many years in opposition becomes a member of Cabinet in Government. There is a change over from attack to defence, and from holding a simple and clear position to being involved in complexities and conciliation. The fire still burned but now in more controlled and harnessed ways. The few Australians who had known or heard him in the old country could see the difference and sometimes wistfully wondered where the vigorous oratory had gone.

Hammond's relationship to Mowll was nonetheless only a working relationship. He was not a close friend of the Archbishop nor part of his social circle, 'Mowll's Court' as it was known. It often annoyed Hammond when, after a hard-working session to bring about change or improvement, some of the Archbishop's friends could get his ear over a cup of tea and add or modify things easily.

A realistic assessment of the situation suggests that Mowll expected too much from Hammond. By making him Principal of Moore College and at the same time rector of an important city church, Mowll was setting him two incompatible tasks. Hammond succeeded at Moore College; but it was beyond any man's capacity also to give St. Philip's the attention it needed. The routine work was done by a succession of curates, while Hammond himself did most of the preaching, even when not scheduled. The work there did not fulfil the potential expected from its presiding place in the city.

'THE PRINC'
The major phases of Hammond's working life fall into three segments of roughly seventeen years apiece: St.

Kevin's, Dublin (1903-19); the Irish Church Missions (1919-36), and now the third stage as Principal of Moore College.

The College, founded in 1856, had served the church in Sydney and beyond. It had always been relatively small, dependent on part-time teachers, under-financed and too closely affected by its Principal's health, domestic arrangements or theology.

This had been very apparent in the case of Archdeacon Davies. He was overworked in the college and in order to earn a living wage he was forced to take on outside work marking examination papers. His wife also taught, as well as being in charge of housekeeping. His openness to liberal scholarship caused concern in Sydney. As far back as just before the Great War he had been attacked at an Australian Church League dinner by the zealous but hasty Everard Digges LaTouche. Indeed it was said that some students were praying for his conversion. The college was described as operating just above stalling speed.

Hammond therefore took over a rundown institution which was in debt, in need of repair, and dispirited. He worked hard at every aspect of college life. He inspired others to join in, and he was a good delegator. With the backing of Archbishop Mowll in major decisions and the steady administrative work of the Vice-Principal, Marcus Loane, compensating for his deficiencies in that area, he enlarged the College and its usefulness. He gave purpose, vigour and intellectual credibility to the work of the lecture room. He upgraded and lengthened the courses; he started extension courses; he instituted daily sermons; he began the annual Conventions; he supervised the improvement of the buildings and the addition of three new wings. During his time the Cash Memorial Chapel was built. He motivated the Women's Auxiliary to supplement the meagre furnishings and domestic necessities.

The College grew numerically, as the annual photographs testify, and its reputation as a centre of educational excellence increased both inside and outside of Anglicanism. Nearly two hundred men were ordained during his years. Out of one class of students three were subsequently made bishops. The College's evangelical ethos was solidly established and sound teaching gave the church in Sydney Diocese a lasting base on which it has been able to build over the years. None of this was easy. Moore College had its share of financial problems and legal difficulties and the Second World War brought its own particular problems of shortage during the middle years of his principalship.

TEACHER

Hammond accomplished all this and more, and in the process gained all but universal approval without losing the peace and joy of his own faith, or his sense of humour. All the while he remained a patient and approachable teacher and counsellor to people both inside and outside of the college. He was fair as a lecturer without being uncommitted. He was never sarcastic. He was always willing to give reference to, and recommend reading on, positions other than those he himself held. One of his students, who would develop a very different theology, says in this respect: 'He seldom failed to give me an appropriate authority who took a point of view exactly opposite to his own.'[4]

As a teacher, Hammond was also courteous, though impatient of poorly thought-out arguments. He also knew that a story can be a good vehicle for communicating truth. Irish tales, recollections of the many people he had met, and what would now be called 'one liners', were generously served up. During one lecture on marriage, he commented: 'Love can do strange things to a man. . . [pause]. . . it has even been known to make some of them wash the back of their necks!' And frequently when referring to learned authorities he would say: 'Professor—— says this, and Doctor—— says this, but the *truth* is . . .'; or 'So-and-so in his book says such-and-such, but he is in heaven now and knows better!'[5]

He had a fine sense of the ridiculous, although this occasionally betrayed him, and some thought his humour could at times border on the coarse. In his *History of Moore College*, Hammond's Vice-Principal, Marcus Loane, described his humour as 'fescennine' (meaning 'scurrilous', 'ribald' or even 'obscene'). When the book was published a somewhat vexed Hammond asked Loane if he knew the meaning of what he had written. Loane simply replied that he did!

Yet Hammond could draw the line and would not let humour become sacrilegious. On one occasion, in chapel, some students wanted to play a joke on a junior. As he did his appointed duty in taking up the collection they carefully piled their coins round the rim of the plate. TC was taking the service and received the coin ornamented plate. He said nothing until the next day—out of chapel—when he made clear his displeasure at any frivolity which marred the public worship of God.

As a teacher he was no innovator. He started no school of theology nor did he give the world fresh insights. He expounded Christian orthodoxy, presenting the historic and classic core of the faith as it has come down through the centuries, serving it up in Anglican dress.

Outside the lecture room but still within the college he was a fatherly figure to the students. From first interview to long after their ordination they trusted him and were encouraged by his warm faith and sound advice. One student remembers protracted questions from other members of the Admissions Panel, such as his views of the inspiration of Ecclesiastes. By contrast Hammond wanted to know only whether he knew his sins were forgiven. Some students recall the consideration Hammond showed them when they were under financial or domestic pressures; others the way he inculcated loyalty to one's rector, and squashed any idea of young curates forming a 'curate's party' in a church. Many recall how the injunctions carried on from his work in Dublin were passed on to generations of Sydney men: 'Define your terms and verify your references.'

Since the material he taught was all available in the writings of those who had gone before him, Hammond's special contribution was his methodology. Leon Morris describes how he attended Hammond privately for tuition. He learned lasting lessons in logical scholarly approaches to material that were foundational to his own widely-recognised and appreciated contribution to evangelical scholarship.[6]

Hammond also involved himself in his students' social pastimes and welcomed them to his home, on occasions even romping round the floor with them in games or party tricks. It never occurred to him to plan or allocate his time; he could not say 'no' to requests to speak or appeals for help. There were even times (notably one involving the Archbishop) when people would call to take him to preach at a service, only to discover that he had forgotten the engagement. But he would go and would preach 'all the better' some said 'for the want of preparation'.

In College chapel his sermon would follow on from the Scripture reading. One morning a student read the wrong passage. Hammond preached on it. On another occasion, during the War, he was reading a chapter of Scripture in a church service when the electricity failed; he merely 'read' on in complete darkness.

Hammond emphasised the vertical character of worship and conducted services with a simple reverence. It was also his nature to act on the precept 'Give to him who asks'. He was often to be seen walking about with 'down-and-outs', and for years he patiently gave valuable time to a manic depressive man who regularly came just to talk to him.

Shortly after his own arrival, true to an earlier promise, he brought out to Australia both Monica Farrell from Dublin and Emily Norbury who had worked for the Irish Church Missions in London. Monica soon threw herself into evangelistic work and continued the strong stand she had taken in Ireland. She brought with her fears (not without some foundation) that she would be abducted and agreed to speak at the Newman Society in Sydney University only if Hammond would come along as a witness. She was vilified by the Roman Catholic Church and Hammond even took up with the Postmaster General the matter of her being slandered on radio. This was nothing new. Back in Dublin when she had been described as a glib-tongued common looking woman, Hammond had said: 'that will be news for her family, most of whom share in her common looks' (many of them were in religious orders!).

As time went by Monica Farrell became more independent and Hammond quietly disengaged himself from her work. Eventually she resigned her organised connections with the Anglican Church to 'follow the Holy Spirit'. She was a well-known figure throughout Australia until her death in March 1982. Carl Hammond spoke at her funeral.

Emily Norbury worked with Monica for a while in 'The Builders', a junior church league which taught the Bible and Reformation principles in parishes in the diocese, using the One Hundred Texts. But Emily's main work was as head of the Deaconess Institution next to Moore College. The Institution, founded by Mervyn Archdall, trained women as deaconesses to serve in the ever-growing work of keeping up with Sydney's population increase. When she came to Sydney Emily was appalled at the poverty of the Institution and set about making it more comfortable. She was a quieter person than Monica and worked well with Hammond. Her death in July 1944 was a heavy blow to him.

7

Australia at Large

Outside the College altogether, Hammond, now generally known as 'TC', was busy in church matters. He was a popular speaker at Bible studies, (one of which, in the city centre, he led up until the week he died), conventions, Reformation rallies, house parties and summer schools. To generations of young people he threw out the challenge to dedicate their powers of intellect to the contemplation of God as the highest use to which the human mind could be put. He was also in demand for regular Sunday preaching and by these means he greatly influenced thousands of Australians.

Robust though Hammond's preaching was, it was always accompanied with great warmth. At conventions and rallies young people rushed to sit at his table for meals and very easily cajoled stories or impromptu autographs from him. He was a popular teacher for the Sydney Preliminary Theological Certificate. He spoke often for the Evangelical Union in Sydney University. In those days before evangelicals had the support of a wealth of good and well-presented evangelical scholarship his contribution was vital. He gave to future church leaders theological substance to nourish the courage of their convictions by demonstrating that evangelicalism had intellectual credibility, and that it was more than pietism.

One professor of philosophy at Sydney University, a Scot called John Anderson, delighted to attack those whom he considered 'naive' in their beliefs, including Marxists and the 'fundamentalists of the Evangelical Union'. A debate was arranged between Hammond and Anderson in 1941 by a then undergraduate, Donald Robinson (later to become Archbishop of Sydney). It has gained a place in the folklore of Sydney.

The two champions debated during two lunch hours, Anderson in general and vague terms, Hammond by seeking to pin down specific points. At one juncture Anderson made a sweeping statement about being able to 'disprove the Resurrection from the New Testament . . . but I haven't got one with me'—an omission a student near the front offered to resolve! The evangelicals were delighted with their representative and believed that the shallowness of the rationalist cause had been shown. Others felt that the two disputants had merely passed each other by like ships in the night. But the boldness of Hammond's defence of the Christian faith gave evangelicals new heart.

Hammond also became very deeply involved in church politics. He became Rural Dean of Balmain (1936), a Canon of the Cathedral (1937), a member of the Standing Committee (1939), Archdeacon without territorial jurisdiction (1949), and for a while acted as Registrar of the Diocese (1955). He was elected a Fellow of the Australian College of Theology thereby gaining an honorary Th.D. He appreciated the honour and did not mind being called 'Doctor', but never suited the gaiters he wore as an archdeacon! He was nominated for the Council of the

Australian College but was not elected.

Not long after his arrival, and possibly because for some his appointment was 'the last straw', a storm blew up in the diocese. The liberal evangelicals and broad churchmen had begun to feel themselves squeezed out of power, particularly after a number of diocesan committees had been filled with evangelicals. They made their complaint known to Mowll in a private 'memorial' (from which they were later known as 'Memorialists'). Their grievance was that church affairs were totally in the hands of inflexible conservative evangelicals, that the diocese was becoming 'monochrome' with no allowance for diversity, and that Moore College was becoming a factory for turning out 'little T. C. Hammonds'. Mowll did nothing publicly at first, but later he issued a detailed letter and questionnaire to each of the Memorialists. It was known that Hammond's hand was behind this. Hammond had made the bullets; Mowll fired them. They refused to reply. Eventually the division became public knowledge. The Memorialists published a booklet *A Plea for Liberty*, but the situation was never resolved.

Both Mowll and Hammond have been criticised for their handling of this situation. There was widespread feeling that a little get-together over tea at Bishopscourt to air grievances would have solved the matter. But it is unlikely that this would have been the case. This was a trial of strength for control of the Diocese. Some of the Memorialists were strong and manipulative men and would not have rested short of changing the evangelical nature of the Sydney Diocese. The treatment of evangelicals in some other Australian dioceses demonstrated how little 'moderate' churchmen were interested in impartial fair play.

THE RED BOOK CASE

Hammond's place as an adviser to Mowll, his reputation as an Irish Protestant, a 'fiery Irish cleric', his place in the corridors of church politics and his own unwillingness to say 'no', all drew him into a lengthy and ultimately hopeless piece of litigation in the Australian Courts. Its one merit was that it helped to clip the wings of those who wanted to subvert the Anglican Church in Australia. It also served to underline the position of the Diocese of Sydney, and this proved to be an important point in subsequent debates about a constitution for the Australian Church.

Such litigation had frequently taken place in England in the second half of the nineteenth century as churchmen tried to resist the intrusions of ritualists and Anglo-Catholics. The shelves of Hammond's study in Dublin had contained bound volumes of the transactions of the Church Association (an Association which Bishop [then Canon] J. C. Ryle had described as being as necessary to the defence of England as the Army and Navy were). Even W. E. Gladstone wrote for them.

The areas of contention were well known: crucifixes and roods, the confessional, altars, the mixed cup, wafer bread, and prayers for the dead. Bewildering to even sympathetic non-Anglicans as these things may be, for embattled Anglicans they were the flags and battle markers of a huge attempt to turn back the Reformation. Hammond himself, as we have seen, had been embroiled in similar cases in Ireland.

The whole case, in the form of the court transcripts, can still be read; it was published in *The Bathurst Ritual Case* by Dashs of Sydney in 1949.[1] Hammond wrote the Preface for the book and even helped to finance its publication. Advised of the possibility of losing this money he arranged to take orders for the book before it was printed!

The basic facts of the Bathurst case were as follows. Bishop Wylde of the neighbouring Diocese of Bathurst in New South Wales, under the pretext of concern about the divergent ways the service of Holy Communion was being conducted in his diocese, drew up a form of service in 1942. He had this printed (it was subsequently called 'The Red Book') for use in the diocese subject to his permission. But he withheld that permission in some parishes where he believed it would be unacceptable.

'The Red Book' permitted the use of decidedly medieval catholic actions such as the ringing of a sanctus bell, making the sign of the cross, and implicitly encouraging belief in 'the real presence' (in the Roman Catholic sense). It was authorised for the parish of Canowindra (pronounced 'Canowndra'). Members of the congregation and others objected. They appealed to Mowll as their Metropolitan Bishop. Mowll advised Wylde to withdraw it, but he refused, and proceedings were commenced through the Solicitor-General.

'It would be tedious to relate all the subsidiary actions which resulted', Hammond wrote in his Preface. In fact the case dragged on for four years, going to the Supreme Court of New South Wales and cost those who took it up a great deal of time and money. Hammond himself gave evidence for a day and a half. The place of the 1662 Prayer Book and the theology of the Lord's Supper were central issues. Broughton Knox, then recently returned from war service as a Naval Chaplain, and on the staff of Moore College, was also called to speak on the legal and constitutional issues, because the case involved the question of whether the

Church of England in Australia was the same as the Church in England and what the nature of the connection was.

Evangelicals involved in such controversies are often open to the counter-charge that they do not themselves adhere to the Prayer Book. This was the line of defence used in the 'Red Book' case. In other contexts the Archbishop had authorised special books differing from the Prayer Book: Scouts and Girl Guides had been given little service books to use; there had been Anzac (Australian-New Zealand Army Corps) services which had omitted parts of the Prayer Book.

The parishioners and their supporters won the major points of their case; when it was appealed they won again. Technically the judgement handed down applied to only a limited number of churches in the diocese, and a new service book (green in colour) was brought out. But a stand had been taken and it had a sobering affect on bishops who thought they were an ecclesiastical law to themselves.

The recent publication of alternative service books throughout the Anglican communion has so liberalised usage that it is unlikely that such a case could ever arise again. Nevertheless it still stands as a beacon for those who will contend for the Reformation character of Anglicanism. Yet it is also another indicator of a church divided against itself. Sadly spiritual energy has to be expended in defensive controversy within the church rather than in conflict with the world.

NEW SOUTH WALES AND BEYOND
Hammond's trenchant evangelical teaching became well known because, throughout his years in Sydney, he wrote regularly for various Christian papers. Through this

medium he encouraged isolated believers in country areas and in other dioceses where evangelical truth was scarce. He was on the editorial board of *The Australian Church Record*, a popular church newspaper, and wrote for it on a wide range of subjects. Some of his articles merit a more permanent form. Other articles were of local and contemporary interest or were about issues which no longer concern the church at large such as 'six o'clock closing' and 'wet' canteens (*i.e.* selling alcohol) for the troops. He also contributed articles to *The Witness*, the organ of the Orangemen, as well as writing to the newspapers in Sydney. On one occasion he took up the case of a woman whom the police brought back to a convent from which she had fled.

Many Sydneysiders who had never met Hammond knew his voice well. In those pre-television days his Sunday night radio broadcasts on 2CH were a regular part of Sydney life. For years he gave talks on a variety of subjects, moral and religious, but mostly on Protestantism as opposed to Roman Catholicism. A digest of these was published as *The Case For Protestantism*. Some of the chapter headings give a good idea of the ground covered: 'Faith and Works', 'Why we reject Transubstantiation', 'Roman Catholics and the Bible', 'Why Confess to a Priest?', 'Blunders of Popes'.

In Australia in the 1930s and 1940s there was pronounced animosity between Protestants and Roman Catholics at both the ecclesiastical and political level. It was the era of Dr Mannix, Roman Catholic Archbishop of Melbourne who typified Irish Catholic nationalism in its militant form. Sectarianism was rife; the Legion of Mary came to Sydney in 1940.

It was well known that a power struggle had developed and certain government departments, notably that of the

Postmaster General, were arenas for it. The position was perhaps half-way between the embitterment of Ireland and the indifferent toleration of England in those days. The Roman Catholics had their 'champion' also, Dr Rumble, who broadcast on Radio 2SM. Eventually by popular demand the broadcast times were so arranged that people could listen to both Hammond and Rumble.

Hammond was an Orangeman. In his long life he had lived only fourteen years in an independent Ireland (1922-36). There had been little attractive or magnanimous about those years immediately following independence. A narrow sectarian Roman Catholic state came into existence, leadership at many levels going to those who were 'out' in 1916 and who were determined to settle outstanding old scores and to prove what good Catholic Irishmen they were. In bondage to their own freedom they wanted to burn everything British, except coal. Even some fire-engines were painted green! In that period, *The Catholic Pictorial* printed the names of ICM supporters in provincial Irish towns. This was tantamount to an invitation to boycott them in their daily work, and to shun them socially.

Living in Sydney, Hammond seemed to be back where he had started, in a harbour city of the Empire. He was not a driving force in the Orange Order and he did not 'walk' with them. But he found their company congenial and he appreciated the opportunities this gave for preaching to men. He was for a long time their Chaplain General and was awarded their Order of Merit in 1947. In 1960 he was elected Grand Master, but never took office. He was also a member of the Ulster Association, though, he was, as he often would say, 'A man of Cork' and therefore a Munster man.

All these associations were cultural and religious rather than geographical. The Irish Associations were a world of Gaelic Athletic Association games and commemorative masses with a whiff of militant Republicanism. Hammond identified with the only Irish connection he could, although perhaps neutrality would have been better in the long run. Sadly, the scriptural truth for which Protestantism should stand too easily becomes identified with Orange politics and degenerates into such party slogans as 'For God and Ulster' which says little about the eternal God of all the nations. Hammond was not a Freemason, although some of his best clerical friends, including Bishop Hilliard and Archdeacon Johnston, were. Perhaps this link, and the fact that he was himself a member of an oath-bound organisation (the Orange Order), meant that he said little about Freemasonry one way or the other.

The work and teaching of T. C. Hammond were by no means confined to Sydney, or indeed to New South Wales, or for that matter to Anglicanism. He travelled throughout Australia often and visited New Zealand three times, before, during, and after the Second World War. He helped a young Australian clergyman, seconded to South Africa, Stephen Bradley (later Bishop Bradley), to draw up a constitution for the Anglican Church there. He was also a frequent speaker in Melbourne and gave heart to many in a city which had a strong evangelical background but where the message was not signalled as clearly as it was in Sydney. He wrote constantly for *Evangelical Action* (formerly *Good Tidings*) a paper with a nation-wide circulation, edited by his friend, W. R. McEwen, a fellow exile, and a Reformed Presbyterian minister.

TC was a popular guest in many homes where he could

enthral with his stories and conversation. He would tilt himself back on the rear legs of his chair, chewing on his moustache, his rich voice changing from a Dublin to a Cork or to an American accent as the funnier moments in his life were retold. Not being gifted musically did not prevent him from singing at times, 'Zucking Zider' being always near the top of his stock of party pieces.

All through these Australian years Gert looked after him quietly, adapting to the climate and also to Australian food and customs. She was shy of the limelight, but a power in the home. They were different personalities; he was prodigal with money, she was frugal and invested; she could be more outspoken, he was more patient. Older than him she could 'mother' a bit. They had their little spats. Their home was not 'open house' to students, but it was there when needed and hers was no small contribution to his work, even if largely unseen. Once on their travels she was asked to fill in a visitors book with a space for 'Hobbies'; where TC had put his as 'reading, badminton, chess', she simply wrote 'looking after hubby'.

The Hammonds were a well-known couple in Sydney. He did not drive a car; indeed he was not at all mechanical. Furthermore, throughout his life he would not use public transport on Sundays. Thus since the College was at one end of down-town Sydney and St Philip's church in the shadow of the Harbour Bridge at the other end, they walked each way through the city centre.

In their slightly dated comfortable clothes the Hammonds passed all the scenes of that flamboyant city's vanity fair. He always wore his clerical collar in public and was often the target of banter and sometimes abuse. But he could give as good as he took.

One day one of Sydney's amiable pagans called out to him that he was a parasite. Hammond returned by calling his man a 'wobbegong', an Australian name for a type of toothless shark. His detractor said: 'Come off it, that's an insult.' To which Hammond replied: 'Oh is it? But I thought that's what we were playing at.'

Another vociferous man, well intoxicated, kept commenting about him in a crowded tramcar. Initially Hammond ignored him, but this only encouraged the flow of words. He drew himself up and said (in his best brogue) 'How dare you address a priest in the church of God like that?'. The man changed his tune and asked forgiveness, whereupon TC replied in nonsensical Latin, 'Oxus Doxus Glorioxus'! There were no more remarks.[2]

THE 1947-8 VISIT HOME
With World War II over and ten years of hard work in Moore College marked up, the Principal was given leave of absence in June 1947. At seventy another man might have looked for retirement, but he made an extended visit to England and Ireland. One purpose of this reflected Mowll's trust in him, for he was to serve as the Archbishop's advisor at the 1948 meeting of Anglican bishops at Lambeth. Marcus Loane acted as Principal during his eighteen months overseas.

Hammond found post-war Europe a sad and straitened place: 'So much for European progress and civilisation when you couldn't get a decent pot of marmalade'. But he did enjoy the experience.

He arrived in time to speak at the Annual Meeting of the IVF in London. He led a mission at Oxford, although without marked success. In himself he was still the same as ever, but younger English evangelicals saw him as 'elderly'. C. S. Lewis invited him to meet some friends and told how on a previous occasion he had primed students with questions to throw at Hammond but had been helped by some of the answers.[3] He spoke at one of the first conferences at The Hayes Conference Centre at Swanwick while its wartime use as a Prisoner of War camp was still evident in the amount of barbed wire around.

Returning to Dublin, he conducted a mission in St Kevin's in which he was assisted by the Rev Bertie Neill, father of Bishop John Neill. Attendances were in the region of 700 and upwards, though possibly many Christians came simply to hear TC for themselves rather than to bring their friends to listen to the gospel. On the final Sunday night the meeting went on so long and the crowds were so slow to leave that Mrs Barton, the Archbishop's wife, telephoned to ask what had happened to her husband!

Hammond also visited Cork and talked endlessly to the small band of his remaining friends. He travelled out to Schull in West Cork and led an extended week-end mission for C. A. B. Williams, a family friend, for which he was joined by his old YM pal, George Bird.

There were other family reunions. His son John was now a headmaster in the Caribbean, but was at home to meet his parents. His second son, 'Chat', viewed a reunion with some apprehension. After his days in the Evangelical Union in Trinity College, Dublin, he had become decidedly 'high' in churchmanship. His father however made no fuss about it, and took part in the services while staying with them. The Lambeth Conference of Bishops came and went, and the extended visit home drew to an end. Hammond paid a final visit to Dublin on his own, and spoke at the Irish Church Missions. A young Mission worker walked him to the mailboat at the North Wall, Dublin, and Hammond left Ireland for the last time. As a treat for Gert he had planned a westward route back to Australia, crossing the Atlantic on the *Queen Mary* before travelling through Canada and then across the Pacific.

They returned to Sydney at the end of 1948. Soon afterwards he told Mowll that he was willing to resign from the principalship of Moore College. But Mowll was reluctant to let him go and so he remained for another five years.

These latter days were full and busy. More students than ever came to Moore, many being ex-servicemen whose studies had been deferred. Post-war reconstruction was in full swing. Immigrants were coming in greater numbers than ever. Sydney went through another convulsive growth stage, and small 'fibro' churches and halls (constructed with wall-board of a compressed asbestos and concrete mixture) were hastily put up in the suburbs. Mowll, no doubt, did not want to see a change of principals at such a time of flux.

But the work load was exceptionally heavy for a man in his seventies. In addition to the normal college responsibilities he was involved in the erection, furnishing, opening and use of the John Cash Memorial Chapel. Built as a memorial to John Cash, an Australian pilot killed in action in 1941, son of Dr Cash of the Australian College of Theology, the chapel was constructed and lovingly fitted out with the finest materials, although not everyone approved of its location. During construction the Cash family were able to increase their giving through the inheritance and subsequent sale of property in Grafton Street in Dublin. The chapel was opened by the Governor General in July 1950 and consecrated in the November of that year by Geoffrey Fisher, the Archbishop of Canterbury. It would later prove too small for the numbers in Moore College and would be rarely used.

If there is one place in Moore College with which TC is particularly associated it is the Cash Chapel. His students remember his early morning sermons (before breakfast!) when TC would, apparently, prepare on his feet. He would cast about for a spark of inspiration, sometimes feeling his way for fifteen minutes before developing his theme in a profound, reasoned, yet warm and devotional manner. Those early morning occasions were unforgettable in a number of ways: the memory of his sermons as well as the marks of the nails of his boots on the parquetry floor at the Lord's Table both remain!

SENIOR CITIZEN

Although now in his seventies, Hammond remained popular, well-loved and in the limelight. The warmth and love in his personality endeared him to Christian people. He remained vigorously active in evangelical causes. He spoke and wrote against the concept of a Catholic University for Sydney (1951)—as did a number of Roman Catholics. He also joined with others on the New South Wales Council of Churches in their protests about some of the territorial claims made by the (Roman Catholic) 'National' Eucharistic Congress in 1953.

Some of his best convention addresses come from this period, including one at Katoomba in 1949 when he shared the platform with his fellow Irishman W. P. Nicholson. For some the Katoomba Convention just 'wasn't "Katoomba" without TC.' But he was not quite so popular with the organisers of the Upwey (Melbourne) Convention, largely because his messages on sanctification stressed practical obedience rather than the looked-for Keswick emphasis on crisis experiences of 'yieldedness'.

Meanwhile Hammond remained involved in the ongoing constitutional debate in the General Synod, defending Sydney's (and therefore every other diocese's) independence. But in 1955, to the disappointment of many of his younger friends, he voted for a draft constitution which fell short of what evangelicals, and others, had been holding out for. In the event, he believed it was the best that was likely to be available. He also fought for, and pushed through, a Vestments Order in 1949 which made illegal certain clerical robes and ecclesiastical terms dear to ritualists. This was an unpleasant debate, lasting for three days, and intemperate words were used. But it wrote into an Ordinance of Synod the prohibition of the chasuble and other sacerdotal vestments. It is still in force.

After the death of Mowll in November 1958, TC opposed the appointment of Donald Coggan (who would become Archbishop of York and later of Canterbury) as Archbishop of Sydney, on the grounds of his alleged departure from the evangelical position on the inspiration of Scripture. In the face of a division among evangelicals, the central churchmen lined up to appoint H. R. Gough (1959-66).

Some time earlier, Lord Wakehurst, the Governor of New South Wales, had approached Mowll and asked him to appoint two clergyman to meet with two senior Roman Catholic clergy to publish an agreed statement on public affairs. Mowll chose Hammond as one of his men and he thereafter met regularly with his Catholic counterparts. One of them was Monsignor (later Archbishop) O'Brien.

However nothing substantial emerged from these discussions before the Governor's term of office had expired.

But the sun was now setting. Hammond's prodigious memory was beginning to let him down in small things. Instead of an opening prayer before a lecture he occasionally prayed in words appropriate only to grace before meals. He himself joked that he had passed from 'dotage to anecdotage'. Whereas earlier students had called him 'the Princ' now he was more often called 'Old Tom'. His reference material tended to be dated, and he would frequently set up and knock down an 'aunt Sally'. The immediate challenge before ministerial students was the rapid advance of hedonistic materialism, but Hammond continued to give lectures at length on the differences between *rite* and *recte*.[4] He dwelt increasingly on sacramental theology and told more stories of nineteenth century Cork. Nevertheless, his solid doctrinal material was still there and many students continued to derive benefit from it. He was given a special celebration for his 75th birthday and he sat, unwillingly, for a presentation portrait.

Hammond resigned from the principalship at the end of 1953, and the arrangement under which Moore College and St Philip's had been yoked together came to an end. This union of ministries had taken much financial strain off the College, and Hammond had willingly donated monies that were rightly his, such as wedding fees (and St Philip's was a very fashionable place to be married) to the College. Now an archdeacon, he continued to lecture at Moore two or three times a week, and remained as Rector of St Philip's. His son-in-law Fred Taplin joined him there, and this help enabled him to continue his speaking ministries and radio work. He proposed the sale of the land on which the rectory stood; an office block now occupies the site.

A Billy Graham Crusade was held in Sydney in 1959. Some of the main-line denominations, blighted by liberalism, would not get involved. It was largely Baptists and Anglicans who gave Graham the support needed. The Crusade had a substantial impact and Anglicanism in particular benefited, a number of later church leaders in Sydney being influenced during it. TC was given a place of honour on the platform and during his stay Billy Graham sought him out for consultation. He was willing to come to Hammond, but TC insisted on going to Graham's hotel so that they would be less likely to be disturbed![5] Hammond thus spanned the era between the two most famous American evangelists of the modern era; the young man who had been at a lunch for Moody in Victorian Cork was now the aged churchman talking with Billy Graham under the Southern Cross.

FRIEND OF THE BATTLE-WEARY SAINT

Hammond enjoyed good health almost to the end of his life. But one day, a couple of years before he died, he and Gert left St Philip's Rectory where they lived, to go into town on business. He had a mild stroke in the street, but, with her dislike of making a fuss or missing an appointment, Gert kept him going until their business was completed, despite the fact that TC was bent to one side. He recovered and kept up a full round of work. He had no thought of retirement. As he put it: 'When I retire my widow will live with my daughter'.[6] He continued to preach, visit, teach and welcome people into the rectory after Sunday evening services.[7] He enjoyed the serenity of a long life lived in the faith of Jesus Christ.

Many saw Hammond only as a controversialist, and it

has always suited some to paint him so. But, in fact, he was a fine Christian, with an extraordinarily able intellect and a well-stocked memory. He was always willing to serve. When compelled to take up controversy on behalf of truth he was always fair and courteous. His grasp of Christian doctrine was immense but his own faith was childlike. Fred Taplin, his son-in-law, once asked him how he slept so well with so much on his mind and so many demands on his time; he replied: 'Well! it's like this, Fred, I say to the Lord —"Here is my day, take what was good and forgive what was bad. Now I am going to sleep." And I do, Fred, I do.'

In September 1961 Hammond was hospitalised for some weeks, but was later able to return to work. On Sunday the 12th of November he took services as usual, but in giving out the announcements for the following week he added: 'These apply to you, but they won't apply to me.'

That Wednesday he had a cerebral haemorrhage. His daughter Doris and her husband Fred were with him; Carl was sent for from Melbourne. Hammond was taken to the City Hospital. He lived for less than an hour. He regained consciousness, thanked the doctors for being so kind, and said: 'I'm going now.' Thus his pilgrimage ended. Death, the king of terrors had been transformed into the 'friend of the battle-weary saint' (to use his own phrase)[8] on the morning of Thursday the 16th of November.

When Carl arrived from Melbourne and went into his father's study he found open on the desk a volume of the Latin writings of the famous 16th century Roman Catholic theologian Robert Bellarmine. TC had spent his last conscious hours preparing his next talk for Radio 2CH. The news of his death soon circled the globe. Newspaper obituaries variously described him: 'one of Australia's most distinguished Churchmen' (*Australian Church Record*); 'a noted theologian and a staunch and outspoken supporter of his Church' (*Irish Times*); 'We naturally mourn his departure from the Church on earth, but thank God that He enabled a faithful man to make such good use of his talents through a ministry of close on sixty years' (*Church of Ireland Gazette*). In Cork his old friend George Bird was told of his death as he was being given a lift home from a YM meeting. He was quiet until he reached his house; as he got out of the car all he said was: 'I'll have to think about this.' A large memorial service was held in Sydney, another in London, yet another in Dublin. A plaque was erected in St Philip's in 1979.

Mrs Hammond lived to be nearly a hundred and died on the 11th of January 1970.

After Hammond's time the teaching at Moore College necessarily developed a different emphasis; dogmatic theology gave way to biblical theology, and in the diocese at large the controversy with Rome and ritualism receded. Evangelicals were more confident and conservative scholarship was beginning to produce its own literature.

The Diocese of Sydney now became less distinctively Anglican and its evangelism was based less on church services. The issue of clerical robes was no longer a question of which robes to wear but of whether to wear any. The 1662 Prayer Book was laid aside or used at early services only. Church leaders looked more to an involvement with South-East Asia than back to the Reformation history of Europe. The idea of the church as an aggregate of society changed and was replaced by an emphasis on the congregation as the gathered people of God. The challenge of late twentieth century evangelism in a materialistic society was manfully faced.

Superficially it could be said that even before he had died Hammond was one of 'yesterday's men'. But if this is true it is so only in the sense that in building a house laying the foundations is inevitably a past event as soon as the house rises above the ground.

Hammond had brought to Australia the trained and well-educated mind of a widely-read and seasoned theologian. He had come when the evangelical cause was weak and lacking in theological depth, and when Roman Catholicism had its eyes set on turning Australia into a Catholic country. He had come when the hollow fruits of modernism and the bitter attacks of ritualism were in danger of changing the character of the Diocese of Sydney, and he had helped to turn back the tide. 'He was a burning and shining light when Australia was under the dark clouds brought about by liberalism in most of the theological schools.'[9] He marked out solid ground for the Diocese of Sydney to build on, and he helped to begin the work of reconstruction in such a way as made it easy for others to follow. Like his father, in different circumstances, he had been a steady hand on the helm during storms.

Wistfully we might ask: What would have happened if he had been allowed do such work in Ireland? But there is another hypothesis to be considered. If, as many believe may be the case, the Diocese of Sydney can help to deliver the world-wide Anglican communion from itself, or, in a bleaker scenario, become the root stock of a reformed Anglicanism, then the work of T. C. Hammond will prove to have been of more than local significance.

8
Books and Theology

Sometime in 1890 Tommy Hammond scribbled his name on the inside cover of the Visitors Book of Cork YMCA and smudged the page as he closed it. It is the oldest extant example of his writing, but happily it was to be followed by four major books, several smaller ones and a host of booklets, as well as contributions to other books and periodicals. (See Appendix I.)

Three of these books he considered 'brothers'. They were published within seven years of his departure from Ireland for Australia (1936-43). While two of them never became well-known, the third, *In Understanding Be Men* became a household name for decades wherever evangelicals began to study theology. It is a basic handbook of doctrine, but based on considerable knowledge and expertise. First produced in the 1930s under the shadow of international disruption, and exported all over the world, it is not only remembered with affection but still in use.

The work went through five editions before being revised by David F. Wright in 1968. It has sold about 150,000 copies and at the time of writing, is still in print. It has been translated into French as *Freres, Je Ne Veux Pas Que Vous Ignoriez* ('Brethren I would not have you ignorant') as well as into Indonesian, Chinese, Czech, Italian, Rumanian, Serbo-Croat, Slovak and Spanish.

Written with university students in mind,[1] it has a strongly didactic tone ('the student will be well advised . . .' p. 35) and is somewhat protective of its student readers ('students need to be on their guard . . .' p. 125). Sometimes it raises and then withdraws a question and is constantly apologising for shortness of space.

The goal of brevity with comprehensiveness led to the multiplication of categories and headings so that the information that Christ redeems from 'all evil' (p. 156) is found as point C. IV. iii. c. group III (5) of the Person and Work of Christ! It also led to the occasional lapse. We are, for example, promised four 'abuses' of Christian ministry (p. 211) but are given only three. Surprisingly Hammond of 'verify your references' fame misquotes Pliny's letter to Trajan about the early Christians singing a hymn to Christ as to God (p. 217).

Early editions had an 'Oxbridge' dust jacket showing gowned students in a college quadrangle. Although not written for theological students but for 'Arts, Science and Medical students', it soon became a standard book in Bible Colleges and for evangelical divinity students and was widely used as a basis for Bible study and correspondence courses. It circled the globe and found its way to every mission field. It brought needed biblical reasoning to an evangelicalism which had become sentimental, subjective, and in some ways inadequate for the times.

One student in preparation for overseas missionary work having attended a Bible College with a strong emphasis on 'holiness' seen largely as an experience, came out knowing little theology and considered it the height of achievement when he was able to live through a week 'without sin'. He soon was in China and was expected to teach Christian doctrine to large Bible classes. He did the only possible thing: he took his students through *In Understanding Be Men*, learning with them.

Many others testify to how the book put backbone into their faith and gave them a theology which informed their minds to replace their earlier vague notions of what it meant to be a Christian.

In Understanding Be Men gives expression to the broad evangelical consensus in theology. It is somewhat Anglican in ethos and mildly Calvinistic in emphasis. In keeping with most pre-World War II literature its author did not feel it necessary to give special attention to teaching about the baptism or gifts of the Holy Spirit. This was not to ignore the work of the Spirit, but rather to see his ministry integrated into the total divine economy.

On those questions where evangelicals differ, for example on baptism, church order and the last things, it gives a few cautious pointers and then refers the reader to larger works. It avoids the temptation to reduce the counsel of God to neat and simple dogmas. With regard to election Hammond says: 'There are some points in the scheme of Christian Doctrine where a "reverent agnosticism" and an earnest attempt to remain faithful to the biblical presentation is far preferable to the production of a completely "water-tight" scheme' (p. 112).

Hammond himself made some changes and corrections for the second edition. The misleading words: 'This removed from our Lord the taint of original sin' (p. 125) were changed to 'our Lord was free from the taint of original sin'. An index was added. Thereafter little was changed (apart from the updating of book lists) until the fourth edition. Partly because there were so few books of its kind available in the United Kingdom, but also because of its own merit, *In Understanding Be Men* held centre stage for a long time and moulded the thinking of generations of Christians. It may be hard for younger Christians today, when such a variety of evangelical literature is available, to appreciate the vital role it played in its first thirty years in strengthening evangelicalism.

PERFECT FREEDOM

Perfect Freedom, which came out in 1938, is a much longer work of 420 pages. TC dictated it to his secretary in short sessions in his busy early days as principal of Moore College. He appears to have been able to pick it out of the drawer whenever a few free minutes arose, saying 'now where were we?' and proceed to dictate. This may explain a few repetitions in it, but it was nevertheless a great achievement.

It is a full and masterly work on ethics written from the standpoint of one trained in classical philosophy. It surveys the history of ethics going back to Plato, before dealing with the Christian ethic and its foundations. Here Hammond is very careful not to set up a legalistic system and any reader seeking merely a list of 'dos and don'ts' will be disappointed: 'It is no part of Protestant Christian Ethics to provide a system of set rules, and it is the glory of the Christian gospel that it has not done so' (p. 19). Instead Hammond shows how Christian behaviour comes from our union with Christ being worked out throughout our lives by the Holy Spirit:

The enabling of the Spirit, which is a portion of the gift secured to us in consequence of our individual relation to God, is a guarantee of final victory even over resident powers of evil. The doctrine of justification by faith thus appears as a perfect ethical motive. It has value because it places the supreme will of God in the right position. It has further value because it represents us as earnestly seeking the fulfilment of that will, and represents God as meeting our inability with a provision that could be found only in the depths of the Divine nature. Self-interest is no longer the dominant principle in our conduct. We have been brought face to face with God, we have trembled before a sense of the inevitableness of His judgement, we have been quickened to hope through the revelation that He has found a ransom, we have been stirred to a loathing of our own condition and induced to yield our members as servants to righteousness. We have peace with God (p. 219).

Perfect Freedom is not an easy book to read but it is a deeply satisfying one. Perhaps because there is so much philosophy in it, or because many Christians prefer to have cut and dried rules of conduct instead of the challenge of spiritual liberty which involves working out ethical decisions from first principles, it was never a popular book and never sold well. It is largely unknown now.

The third of the 'brothers' was *Reasoning Faith*, published in 1943. This was an ambitious attempt at apologetics seeking to set out a strong and reasonable case for Christianity. It covers philosophical, scientific and historical objections to the Christian faith and brings under scrutiny questions as diverse as material monism, Bertrand Russell's epistemology, evolution and form criticism.

It leaves the reader with two impressions: the breadth of Hammond's knowledge of non-theological subjects and the shallowness of many of the standard objections to Christianity.

Hammond may have cast his net too wide and the specialist in any one area would, no doubt, look for a fuller treatment of issues. Yet the work exploded the myth that evangelicals were, by definition, anti-intellectual. The nature of many of the scientific questions raised in *Reasoning Faith* mean that it would require updating if it were to keep pace with new discoveries. Hammond himself was well aware of this and a copy of the book in Moore College library is interleaved with his own additions.

Of interest among his smaller books is *Fading Light* published in 1942. It contains a series of lunch hour talks in St Philip's Church, Sydney. Although the subject—Nazi Germany—may be dated, the argument goes far beyond its immediate application and is relevant to every situation in which a human philosophy usurps the place of God in the life of a nation. Here Hammond traces the steps of decline and irrationality that lead away from God to the deification of man.

Another book of similar size, *Age-Long Questions* (originally given as the Gunther lectures in St. Andrew's Cathedral, Sydney), is more peripheral. It is a work in the philosophy of religion and is based on the approach of Bishop Butler's *Analogy of Religion*, of which Hammond was marking the two hundredth anniversary of publication. Butler, sometimes remembered only for his denunciation of John Wesley's enthusiasm, sought to defend Christianity against deism on the grounds of 'probability', the common sense theory of being sure of certain things accepted by common men regardless of the subtle arguments of philosophers.

From Hammond's earlier days came two books which were largely overlooked although both made statements which acted as correctives to popularly-held conceptions. In *Penal Laws* he analysed the idea that the Penal Laws imposed on Roman Catholics were simply sectarian and anti-Catholic religious laws. He traced the matter back to the Reformation settlement in England and subsequent papal pronouncements made against Elizabeth I, when Pius V issued the Bull 'Regnans in Excelsis'. This Bull read in part:

We do, out of the fulness of our Apostolic power, declare the aforesaid Elizabeth, being a heretic, and a favourer of heretics and her adherents in the matters aforesaid, to have incurred the sentence of anathema, and to be cut off from the unity of the body of Christ. And, moreover, we do declare her to be deprived of her pretended title to the Kingdom aforesaid, and of all dominion, dignity and privilege whatsoever . . . And we do command and interdict all and every the noblemen, subjects, people and others aforesaid, that they presume not to obey her or her ministers, mandates and laws; and those who shall do the contrary, we do strike with the sentence of anathema. (cited, p. 56)

In other words the Pope had pronounced an anathema on any citizen who obeyed the government. Hammond proceeds to show that the penal laws against Roman Catholics were a response to the inherent disloyalty and rebellion which such papal pronouncements fostered. He further proved that they were an attempt to prevent Roman Catholics from combining with England's enemies rather than an attack on Roman Catholicism as such.

His *Authority in the Church* arose from a case before the Court of the General Synod of the Church of Ireland.[2] In this book Hammond returns to the early church to demonstrate how bishops gradually assumed a power and authority which never rightly belonged to their office. The book is not a denial of episcopacy but an attack on usurpation and autocracy in the church. It is very closely argued, and unanswerably so. But the work never received the circulation it deserved.

Paradoxically, Hammond is usually given more credit than he actually deserves for his next major work. The popular conception that he wrote *The Hundred Texts* is not the full picture. As we have noted already, he revised an existing work which had last been issued by Henry Fishe in the 1880s.

Hammond prepared and published the first fifty texts (1927) and then hurriedly completed the remaining fifty during the period of his move to Australia. The whole work was published after his departure, having been typed on the first typewriter the Mission purchased. He tidied up and amplified Fishe's work and produced, in catechetical form, a miniature encyclopaedia of the main differences between Roman Catholicism and the teaching of the churches of the Reformation.

He changed Fishe's edition in a number of ways. He rejected Fishe's assertion that baptism with the Holy Spirit was a distinct second work in Christian experience and also differed from his position on sanctification. *The Hundred Texts* is a most useful teaching book with good methodology and copious references. It serves as a reminder of the stark contrast between biblical teaching and Roman Catholicism. In 1956 Mabel Tector an Irish missionary in Qua Iboe brought out an abridgement of *The Hundred Texts* for use on the mission field; but a revised full edition, taking Vatican II into account, is needed.

THE NEW CREATION

Hammond's last major writing, and in some ways his best, was *The New Creation* (1953). It is a work of inductive biblical theology. The theme is regeneration which he fully expounds in relation to faith, conversion and justification. He outlines different views on justification, traces the various strands in sanctification and looks forward to glorification. It is the mature fruit of a lifetime of study and a book to which the student will want to return for an accurate understanding of fine theological distinctions.

Many of his booklets and pamphlets were of a topical and passing nature and were mostly in the area of the Roman Catholic controversy, but a few encapsulated much of his theology in a simple homely style such as *The Way of Salvation*, *So Great Salvation*, *Evangelical Belief* and *A Catechism on the Church Catechism*.

Hammond's writings reflected the width of his interests and varied from the popular and ephemeral to the philosophical and scholarly. He could give folksy illustrations and joke with his readers. He could also make them reach for a dictionary with words like 'subreption', 'ataraxy', and 'amphibology'. New writers and publishers now supply the Christian reader, and so it must be. But much of what Hammond wrote had a timeless quality displaying a deep wisdom and an understanding of both biblical theology and human nature which still serves as a good counter-balance to the over-subjective theology and the experience-centred autobiographies which tend to dominate popular Christian publishing.

T. C. Hammond was not an innovator; he had no new insights nor was he the guru of a new school of theology. He handed on what he had received and contended for 'the faith once for all delivered to the saints'. He held firmly to the biblical teaching on, and experienced personally, assurance of forgiveness and the believer's secure place 'in Christ' based on the Saviour's finished work.

Hammond took, used and explained all that was best in the past. After Scripture itself he knew, valued and distilled the Fathers and the Reformers along with the episcopal tradition represented by Ussher in theology and Butler in apologetics.

Sometimes described as a polymath, Hammond was certainly an all-rounder in knowledge—legal, philosophical, historical, biblical and dogmatic. Consequently his theology was well-rounded and informed, never descending to the narrow or eccentric. While he grew as a theologian, his basic beliefs remained constant, his earliest setting out of theology in digest form in *A Catechism on the Church Catechism* (*c.* 1912) has the same evangelical teaching as one of his last statements in 1956 in *What is an Evangelical?*

The doctrine of justification by grace was the cornerstone of his faith and his teaching. He taught that we are accounted righteous and thereby justified exclusively on the basis of our Lord's atoning work. When explaining justification he simply quoted the words of the Westminster Confession, Article 11 of the Thirty-Nine Articles and the Homily on Justification.

Only in *The New Creation* does he expand his understanding of justification by discussing in depth its relation to regeneration. He rejects the view of his seventeenth century namesake, Henry Hammond, who taught that we are saved by the death of Christ *and* the fulfilment of those obligations God lays upon us. Knowing that our salvation is in Christ and therefore apart from our own efforts or merit he glories in the reality of the assurance which the believer can enjoy, and be motivated by, here and now.

While Hammond's theology was certainly Anglican, it was never stretched to become 'Anglican right or wrong'. He was very much at home in mainstream evangelicalism. He was not a 'fundamentalist' in the modern pejorative sense of the word. He did not tie the 'days' of creation to twenty-four hour days. He believed in the verbal inspiration of Scripture but was careful not to interpret that in any 'mechanical' sense. He supported with due caution the re-marriage of innocent parties to divorce.

Having been forged on the streets of Cork and honed by quick-witted heckling in Dublin his theology never lost sight of the common man or of the need of redemption in Christ. Consequently his messages and addresses were human and relevant. This was why he was so popular and effective as a speaker, even in his old age in Australia. One Sydney teenager said in later life: 'He was the first person who made me laugh in church'.

With his background in disputes with Roman Catholicism TC was particularly strong on areas of theology where there were significant differences. This was especially the case in sacramental theology. Unfortunately his work in this area was largely dissipated into small booklets and radio talks, although he may well have intended to write something in this field since a short typescript exists. He was precise in his understanding of the Lord's Supper, rejecting the 'bare memorial' doctrine of many evangelical fellowships:

Protestants are badly misrepresented because they deny that they take the very body of Christ into their mouths. They are charged with making the Holy Communion a mere symbol. What they try to teach is that the bread in the sacrament remains bread and the wine remains wine. But our Lord has given to these outward symbols a new meaning. They represent His body broken and His blood shed and if we take them in faith as such representations our Lord Jesus Christ makes us sharers in all that His body and blood secured for us. We feed upon Him in our hearts by faith.[3]

Baptism he regarded as a sign of membership and, when accompanied by faith, a seal of union with Christ; as an extension of this he accepted infant baptism in the context of its covenantal significance, but vigorously rejected the idea of regeneration *ex opere operato* (*i.e.* simply by the proper performance of the rite). His theology of baptism also contained elements of the view that an established church has a certain responsibility for all citizens.

Hammond had no interest in speculative prophecy; nor was he enthusiastic about the ecumenical movement, believing that any union which did not have a thoroughly biblical basis would simply be like two pools, the higher of which would inevitably drain into the lower. For him spiritual unity was more significant than any external uniformity.[4] In an age in which experience tended to outweigh thought among evangelicals, TC emphasised the vital role of the mind in Christian believing and was impatient of shallow emotionalism or unthinking belief:

The fundamentals of the Christian faith have not been taught with sufficient care for years. As a result the youth of our day are often ill-instructed. We have too many purveyors of a cheap Gospel which makes its appeal solely to the emotions and does not supply a solid background of Bible fact on which the awakened soul may confidently rest.[5]

Wherever religion is based on feelings and an irrational

appeal to inner voices the need for a reasoned biblical faith is evident. The choice of the text 'in understanding be men' (*1 Cor.* 14:20 A.V.) as the title for a handbook on Christian doctrine was by no means haphazard.

Always fair to those who disagreed with him, Hammond gave to his students and readers the option of consulting writers from differing viewpoints. Even in the realm of debate with or discussion about the Church of Rome he readily acknowledged truth where it was found and never descended to the cheap jibes, distortions and petty insults beloved of some Protestant leaders. He would have regarded that as playing to the gallery rather than rightly handling biblical truth.

Although he spent years in face to face confrontation with Roman Catholics he could never be charged with bigotry. He knew the difference between intolerance and indifference and was realistic about error. But he spurned the carnal weapons of the demagogue.

Hammond was at the height of his powers in the late 1920s and 1930s when evangelicals were not particularly numerous in the field of scholarship. The coming of the effects of higher criticism to the man in the pew in the early decades of the century had for a time jolted evangelicals. Some remained silent, most retreated to the safe inward-looking world of a devotionally-orientated rather than a robustly doctrinal faith. The old guard from the days of Victorian confidence, the men of Hammond's youth: D. L. Moody, R. A. Torrey, H. G. Moule, J. C. Ryle, F. B. Meyer had gone to their reward. The men who were to become the leading evangelicals in Hammond's old age—F. F. Bruce, Billy Graham, Leon Morris, John Stott—were still at school or university.

Along with a very few others Hammond kept, defended, commended, lived out and passed on the faith through a period when evangelicalism was theologically weak. This and the intellectual strength of his theology are probably his greatest contributions.

9

Ireland After Hammond

M any others beside Hammond saw Ireland's need of the gospel. Similar zeal has characterised numerous other Christians during the twentieth century. The main Protestant denominations had 'Home Missions' or 'Irish Missions' and individual clergymen engaged in outreach. But they were in a minority in the Church of Ireland as well as in the Presbyterian and Methodist Churches. Sadly, many members of these denominations had little understanding of the privileges and responsibilities of the gospel for themselves and therefore were not concerned about the need of their fellow countrymen. Equally sadly, many ministers were muted because they had absorbed the modernism of their college training and had lost sight of the vitality and urgency of the Christian message.

In the 1920s Irish Protestants were still living with the recent memory of shootings and burnings (140 country houses had been burned in 1922-3). They were now part of an isolated minority of less than seven per cent of the population. The common policy was to be quiet, give no offence and 'keep your head down'. Nor was this without cause. For most of the century every Protestant in the South was aware of a smouldering hostility of long-held hatred which lay just below the surface. While historically understandable, this hatred had been freshly fuelled for party political or religious reasons and kept alive for new generations by some teachers in Irish schools.

It surfaced in different ways. Protestant children had to be allowed out of school earlier than Roman Catholic pupils in order to be off the streets and out of harm's way. *Corpus Christi* processions virtually reduced the streets of whole towns to outdoor Catholic churches with public worship of the sacramental wafer. A shop assistant who did not call a priest 'Father' was told ' 'twould be better for you if you'd never been born'. Local political meetings, social organisations and sporting bodies all had priests in honorary positions thereby freezing out Protestants from community life.

Protestants who offended in any of the minor matters of daily living such as a place in a queue, a minor traffic accident, wartime rationing, job prospects or promotion, soon found that the religious dimension was introduced and aired vociferously. Some incidents, by no means the worst, gained national attention: the boycott of Protestants in Fethard-on-Sea over a domestic marriage problem; discrimination against a Protestant librarian in County Mayo was defended in the Irish Parliament, the Dail, by de Valera; a church in Kilmallock and an Irish Church Missions home in Tipperary were burned in the 1930s. The pressure was constant. Roman Catholics were forbidden from going to Protestant church services, even for weddings or funerals, under penalty of mortal sin. Similar restrictions applied to attending Trinity College.

Not surprisingly only the most motivated members of

the main Protestant churches actively evangelised their countrymen. The smaller and more evangelical churches or fellowships made efforts out of all proportion to their size. Baptist evangelists and pastors preached at fairs and markets. The Christian Brethren maintained a constant witness in the cities and towns of Ireland. The Faith Mission conducted evangelistic services wherever they could get the use of a building or a field.

There were heroic individuals too, who went out to preach the gospel virtually alone. In the 1930s and 1940s, under the auspices of the Dublin YMCA Evangelisation Scheme, Johnny Cochrane, with Victor Evans, and later Arthur Rayner, missioned in nearly three quarters of the Irish counties, at times with police protection and sometimes with a guard dog outside their caravan. The Stuart Watt sisters, following their father's example carried on a loving, if somewhat individualistic work that took them into the darkest parts of Dublin city.

This was the situation when Hammond left Dublin in 1936, and neither the years of the Second World War nor of the 1950s brought much change.

Overseas missionaries and Pentecostals took up the task from the mid-century on. Stanley Mawhinney from County Down, who worked at first with the European Missionary Fellowship, evangelised in market towns and opened a series of book shops which were beacons of light. The list could go on, those named must stand as representative of many more unnamed.

An event in 1958 marked the end of the old days. Three Irish evangelists had held an open-air meeting in Killaloe. There was some agitation and the police advised them to leave. On the way back to their car they were set upon and one of them was knocked unconscious. Up to this point it might well still have been 1858. But the police prosecuted the assailant. The national papers took up the case claiming that the attack had been dealt with too lightly in the courts and defended the right to preach unmolested. The case's greatest significance was that it marked the demise of open violence and drew from the Court a recognition of the need for a freer, more open society.

THE 1960s

By the 1960s the number of Irish evangelicals had dropped to a low point as the old generation died out. On one occasion no one except the preacher came to a service in Cork Baptist Church. However, a number of factors were already afoot that were to bring widespread change.

To trace the hand of God in these events lies beyond our present scope. The 'Troubles' in the North certainly put Ireland on many prayer lists. Among traceable influences, however, was that of the media. Most of Ireland's east coast could receive English television, and this in turn encouraged the sales of popular English tabloid newspapers. Both broke down the isolationist and strongly Roman Catholic culture. Emigration slowed down as a result of economic growth and exiles began to return, bringing more liberal attitudes of life with them.

The changes introduced by Vatican II had an effect profounder than the Council's documents themselves would suggest. Down through the years the idea that the Roman Catholic Church never changes had been used as a bulwark defence against Protestant diversity. The 'True Church' was ever and always the same. This continuity was typified for most Catholics by the Latin liturgy and the eating of fish on Fridays. Now these old unchanging features were disappearing.

The changes themselves were hardly radical, but they were changes. Once the possibility of change is admitted an irreversible process begins. Politicians now spoke out increasingly against the influence of the Catholic Church. With the setting up of the Irish Free State in 1921 the role of the Church changed. For centuries she had benefited from being identified with the people against England, the landlords and the Protestants, so much so that she could hardly do any wrong. Now she had become the *de facto* established church. Politicians ruled with one eye on Maynooth, where the major seminary was. This was inevitable when politicians were themselves Catholics, and priests and nuns shaped the political thinking and influenced the votes of many.

In 1951 a Coalition Government intended to introduce a mild welfare improvement but ran head-on into doctrinaire objections from the Catholic Church. The Minister for Health was summoned before the Archbishop of Dublin and told to drop the scheme. He resisted but his Cabinet colleagues faltered and abandoned the scheme, one member doing so 'because he didn't want to get a belt of a crozier'. The Health Minister was thus left in isolation.

But the Church's victory was a pyrrhic one. A corner had been turned, and the supposed 'Church of the people' was recognized as being so no longer. The politicisation of issues grew. Irish television made its appearance in time to take up matters long unspoken in public. Discussion programmes and popular shows broke one taboo after another. Amorality became fashionable. Doors were opened which would admit things good as well as things questionable.

The romantic vision of a Catholic and Gaelic rustic Ireland, immune from corrosive influences, re-creating the stirring days of her mythological heroes and self-sufficient in the simple things of life, was now gone forever. The twentieth century had come to Ireland, albeit fifty years late.

In this changing situation two more factors deepened the complexities of Christian witness. The eruption of 'the Troubles' in Northern Ireland in the late 1960s steadily polarised the two communities and again confused the political and religious issues.

Although Protestants in Northern Ireland have a worthy record of missionary service overseas, they do not have a good record for outreach, or even the reaching out of hands, to their Roman Catholic neighbours. The events of recent years in their chilling horror and brutality could not be expected to change this. Leading Protestants fell back on non-biblical attitudes of triumphalism and 'what we have we hold' and fostered, for their own ends, out-of-date notions of conditions in the Republic. Too few asked themselves whether the spread of the gospel throughout all Ireland should not be a greater priority than their idea of political Unionism.

About the same time as these developments the charismatic movement emerged and began to gain ground. Numbers of Irish people had their faith vitalised; but some mistakenly sought short-cuts to holiness and maturity. Others put the emphasis on what could be gained from God rather than what could be done for God. The movement went through a very open phase at first and was welcomed by many as revival and a true work of the Holy Spirit upstaging the failing ecumenical movement. As time went by it took on a more Roman Catholic hue in its major membership. Nevertheless, this had side effects in terms of a new spirit of openness and an interest in Bible study and the spawning of small groups with an emphasis on biblical truth.

NEW BELIEVERS

It is in this context that the emergence of a small but significant number of new believers emerging from a Catholic background and forming themselves into fellowships and churches should be seen. Some heard evangelistic messages on the radio, others were witnessed to by organised outreach teams. Some obtained Bibles and came to the knowledge of the truth unaided, while others observed relatives who had become believers and were convinced. Others again were visited on their doorsteps by local evangelical churches. A recurring note in the testimony of such people were statements such as, 'and when it happened I was convinced that I must be the only Christian in ———.' These individuals soon came together in small groups, or met with longer-established believers.

Incidental things happened which revealed deeply-ingrained cultural differences. Some new believers cut out the page mentioning King James from the front of their Authorised Version of the Bible. When they bought Bibles they avoided black ones since these were identified with Protestants. On the other hand, there was less emphasis on some of the distinctives long cherished by older believers, such as not wearing make-up or purchasing Sunday newspapers.

Furthermore, to these new Christians the use of wine at meals was not a shibboleth, and dressing up for church was no longer *de rigeur*.

The huge question of church membership and loyalty demanded attention. It had been little more than an academic matter in days of small numbers of believers with a Protestant background. They had evolved a dual-loyalty system by which they went to their family church on Sundays as usual and to a 'wee meeting' run by some of the evangelical agencies mid-week for fellowship. But now it became a very live issue.

Some new believers were integrated into Protestant churches, where these were evangelical and welcoming. Some established healthy outward looking independent evangelical churches. Some joined Pentecostal congregations or Brethren assemblies. Some met in their homes unsure of who they were or what they believed about their relationship to organised groups of Christians. Yet others were influenced by more esoteric leaders, both native and cross-Channel, and formed rather isolationist fellowships. Many disillusioned, untaught and confused slipped back and lost interest. In this situation of enormous flux, mistakes were doubtless made. Older believers sometimes failed to distinguish between their own religious traditions and essential biblical truth, and thus caused offence to keen new converts. On the other hand, some new converts failed to see past their pre-conversion notions of Protestants and spurned fellowship with them, no matter how evangelical and welcoming they might be.

These problems caused much heartache and damaged Christian witness. But those who had been long engaged in evangelism were able to see that they were at least signs of life. It was now clear to those who knew the Irish situation that a profound change was beginning to take place. For centuries, with very few exceptions, evangelism was something done to the Catholic majority by a small band of zealous believers from the Protestant minority. It had been an unwritten rule that those who were converted would adopt not only the theology of the evangelists but the concomitant life style, church structures and politics. As a result, new Christians tended to be better prepared to serve Christ *outside* of the Irish culture rather than *within* it.

The worthy efforts of the past had been merely a swelling on the Irish body politic; at times a large and fiery one, but never really a movement 'of' the people. This is now changing. New believers, brought up as Roman Catholics and completely one with the majority in culture, are now either forming their own church structures or, where they have found a spiritual home among older Protestant churches, are contributing to their revitalisation from within. Older believers from Protestant backgrounds in the Republic have usually welcomed this, refreshed by the zeal and simplicity of converts and indeed glad to be freed themselves from traditions which were religio-cultural rather than biblical. Between 1970 and the early 1980s many new believers went through an intense time of feeling their way. There was much trial and not a little error. Issues, which in other times had taken decades to work out, were sometimes treated too casually by new converts, who, through no fault of their own, had little knowledge of Scripture and no training in theology. Baptism, church order and teaching about the Holy Spirit were all keenly debated.

Sometimes young people who had been converted only a matter of weeks previously were thrust by force of circumstances into positions of leadership. Evangelicals from North and South, who should have known better, were so delighted by what they saw happening that they tended to lionise converts and set them on shaky pedestals, forgetting pastoral wisdom, church order and discipline in their welcome. Occasionally the same converts were being claimed by different evangelistic agencies; sadly, some converts adopted a loose attitude to church life and fellowship, wandering in and out at will. Denominationalism also came in for heavy criticism. Understandably, most converts, having been misled by the Church of their youth, viewed with suspicion any formal grouping and looked for their own answers. But some of the answers arrived at were not a solution to denominationalism so much as seeds of new 'non-denominational' denominations. The simplistic appeal of the statement, 'We are not the only Christians but we want to be Christians only' sometimes led to forms of Christian nihilism and occasionally camouflaged sophisticated power structures. In the worst cases a few people who had left one Church with a Pope were fast becoming popes in their own fellowships.

Nevertheless it was a springtime of hope. After early mistakes and excesses many settled down to work, love and live as responsible informed Christians. Old church constitutions were studied, the lessons of the past were appreciated and lingering barriers between believers from the two communities in the Republic were being dissolved. Long established evangelical para-church agencies like Scripture Union and The Universities and Colleges Christian Fellowship (formerly Inter-Varsity Fellowship) quickly geared themselves for new spheres of service and were a benefit to new believers, while at the same time they themselves gained greatly from their zeal, freshness and spontaneity.

A number of American missions such as Campus Crusade were also very active. The very increase in the number of college Christian Unions in the Republic—from one in the 1950s to over twenty in the 1990s—is a good yardstick of the change. Comparable statistics would apply to bookshops selling evangelical books.

The smaller, largely evangelical denominations also responded well and have seen integration and growth. In the mainline denominations evangelism gets low priority and ecumenism, relativity in morals, and socio-political issues tend to be given a higher profile. The Presbyterian Church has some ministers of vision in the Republic and is already seeing both spiritual and numerical growth. Some good things have also happened in these same respects in Methodist congregations.

Sadly, Hammond's own denomination, the Church of Ireland, which in some ways 'bore the heat of the day', did little to live up to the implication of its name. Its leadership had developed a strongly ecumenical approach that either did not see the spiritual need which was being expressed or was offended by any suggestion that there is a need to evangelise. Retreat rather than advance marked her role in the Republic. While her dignitaries shared out ancient titles among a decreasing number of clergy, closed churches bore witness to a tide that was going out.

In Northern Ireland the Church of Ireland is stronger, busier and has a sizeable evangelical minority, but immediate pre-occupations take away from any vision of growth in the Republic. Political Protestantism is a very great hindrance. Fresh vision will be needed to prevent an atrophied southern branch falling away from the Anglican Church in Northern Ireland. Men like Hammond would be astounded to see so little being done in days of such opportunity.

OLD MESSAGE . . . NEW MESSENGERS

The evangelists of the past worked under great disadvantage. Even when they were Irish born and reared there was a distance between them and the Roman Catholic majority. In a dozen small ways their Protestant background marked them out: dress, name, hobbies, ethical standards, schools attended, sports followed, accent, and other details. Even where definite efforts were made to off-load cultural Protestantism, with a finely-honed skill any Irish person could still tell the difference. Sadly, and with depressing monotony, the question 'What do you think of Christ?' soon became 'What do you think of O'Connell?' (or Parnell, or 1916, or Ian Paisley).

New believers in the Republic have no such problem. They are not standing on the outside of the society; they belong on the inside; they are 'of' the people. Instead of witnessing to strangers who happen to share the same island, they are dealing with family and friends. After the centuries of effort, these new believers are the best hope for Ireland and are her best evangelists. They are still pioneers, but given the widespread reading of Scripture and the free discussion of the faith among Roman Catholics they could lead where thousands will follow. But care will have to be taken to prevent the growing church in the Republic from being destroyed by deadness in large denominations or by fragmentation into small groupings.

In any and all circumstances the solid, reasoned theology of such as T. C. Hammond will serve the Irish church well. Too often Christians are taught to opt for, or themselves lean to, one strand in theology: reason and bookishness, *or* catholicity, *or* social concern, *or* evangelism. Here Hammond stands as a fine model to follow. He wove all these elements together into a unified, biblical world view. Without becoming rationalistic he worked from a well-reasoned base and could meet the thinker on his grounds. Without capitulating to either Roman or Anglo-Catholicism he was an expert on the Fathers and knew and defended his place in the centre of the historic Christian faith.

T. C. Hammond was truly catholic in the sense of holding to what has been believed by the Christian church at all times and in all places. In addition, without any diminution of evangelistic zeal his concern for the waifs of Dublin or the troubled of Sydney was rooted in a genuine concern for them as individuals, and not merely as fodder for his own cause. Without becoming narrow, obscurantist or shrill he never lost the urgency of the faith in Christ crucified which he came into and preached in Victorian Cork, defended in Dublin and taught in Sydney.

As a man well into his twenties when Queen Victoria died and in his mid-forties when Ireland gained independence TC was pro-Empire; as someone who had seen the machinations of Irish Roman Catholicism at her zenith he supported Protestant causes all his life. But he was too big to come under any master but Christ and too perceptive to follow any cause uncritically. He would surely have taken present changes in Ireland in his stride, with joy.

There was an old tradition in rural Ireland that the fire in the hearth was never allowed go out. Each night it was banked up and in the morning raked over and the new fuel kindled from the hot ashes. This continuity was taken a step further when a new cottage was built. Then the embers were taken from the old hearth to kindle the new fire. Similar continuity has been achieved in the Irish church to which T. C. Hammond devoted part of his life and many of his prayers.

Appendix I

The Writings of T. C. Hammond

T. C. Hammond had a ready pen and was convinced of the need to communicate. From the outset of his ministry until its conclusion he wrote for the public: books, booklets, leaflets, articles, and letters to newspapers. Although he did not exercise any distinct ministry through letter writing, as some Christian leaders have done, he was always ready to write letters in the course of his work.

Most of his booklets were written to respond to issues of the day. While many were in the area of controversy with the Roman Catholic Church, others were the substance of convention talks and provide wholesome biblical teaching. Probably some of these have been lost, and the following list does not claim completeness. Publishing details for many of the booklets are very scant, many of them are undated (nd.), and the list only approximates to a chronological order.

A. BOOKS AND SUBSTANTIAL BOOKLETS:
Authority in the Church, Dublin, 1921. An examination of the position and jurisdiction of the bishops in the Anglican communion.
The One Hundred Texts, London, 1927. The first fifty texts.

Concerning Penal Laws, Dublin, 1930.
In Understanding Be Men (6 editions), London, 1936-68. A synopsis of Christian doctrine for non-theological students.
Perfect Freedom, London, nd. [1938]. An introduction to Christian ethics.
The One Hundred Texts (6 editions), London, 1939-62. The 100 texts used by the Irish Church Missions, with questions and notes.
Age-Long Questions, London, nd. [1942]. An examination of certain problems in the philosophy of religion.
Fading Light, London, nd. [1942]. The tragedy of spiritual decline in Germany.
Reasoning Faith, London, 1943. An introduction to Christian apologetics.
So Great Salvation, Melbourne, 1943.
The Way of Holiness, Melbourne, 1952.
The New Creation, London, 1953.

B. BOOKLETS:
The New Theology (on Campbellism), Dublin, 1907.
Christian Science, Dublin, nd.
The Principles of a Protestant, Dublin, 1909 (a sermon preached in St Kevin's in reply to H. R. Benson).
Immanence and Transcendence, Dublin, nd. [1911].
Bible Truth and Modern Knowledge, nd.
A Catechism on the Church Catechism, Dublin, nd. [1912].
Authority in Religion, 1916.
Authority in Religion, II, 1917.
The Cross on the Communion Table, Belfast, 1917.
Priesthood, Ministry and Apostolic Succession, Dublin, nd.
What is Millennial Dawn Theology?, Dublin, nd.
Triumph Through Christ, Dublin, nd.

How the Roman Church treats the Bible, Dublin, 1921.

Did Protestants Rob Churches?, Dublin, nd. [1920s?]. On the title of the Church of Ireland to its churches.

Dishonest Controversy and Flagrant Intolerance, Dublin, nd. [1920s?].

The Irish Bishops and the Reformation, Dublin, nd. [1920s?].

Reply to Bishop Cohalan's Pastoral, Dublin, 1925. On a mistaken interpretation of justification by faith.

Doubts of the Sons, Dublin, nd. [1920s?]. An answer to Cardinal Gibbon's *Faith of Our Fathers*. This is the best example of the range and force of controversy with the Church of Rome as conducted by Hammond at the peak of such work.

A New Year Sermon (on Isaiah 6:8), Dublin, nd. [1925].

Does the Doctrine of Transubstantiation involve Material Change?, Dublin, nd. [1920s?].

Reformation and Modern Ideals, Dublin, 1927. Lectures given on his first Australian visit.

The Go Preachers, nd. A leaflet on Cooneyites.

Simple Investigation of Great Truths, nd.

Who is the True Pope?, nd. An historical study of gaps in Papal succession.

Evangelical Slogans, London nd. [1928].

Bible Truth and Modern Fancies, nd.

The Fascination of the Church of Rome, nd.

Protestants and the Church of Christ, Dublin, 1932. A reply to Cardinal MacRory's Lenten Pastoral.

Evangelical Revival and the Oxford Movement, London, nd. [1933?].

From the Manger to the Throne, nd. [1930s?].

Inspiration and Authority, London, 1935.

Marriage, My Choice, Dublin, 1936.

The XXXIX Articles, A Safeguard against Romanism, Dublin, nd. [1936].

A Vindication of John Foxe the Martyrologist, nd.

Walking with God, nd. [1940s?].

Good News for Bad Men, nd. An evangelistic booklet.

Can We Advance and Still Believe the Bible?, nd.

Pivotal Points in Revelation, nd.

Subsidising Revolt, nd. On State aid to denominational schools.

Sunday Amusements, nd. Reprinted from *The Australian Christian Review* for 7 May 1942; [1940s?].

How and Why we keep Sunday, nd. Printed from Hammond's broadcasts on Radio 2CH.

How the Reformation Saved the Church of Rome, nd. Printed from Hammond's broadcasts on Radio 2CH.

Confession, nd. Printed from Hammond's broadcasts on Radio 2CH.

Conflict of Faith and Works, nd. Printed from Hammond's broadcasts on Radio 2CH.

Mass, nd. Printed from Hammond's broadcasts on Radio 2CH.

Purgatory, nd. Printed from Hammond's broadcasts on Radio 2CH.

Light and Life, nd. Talks given at the Upwey Convention 1942-43.

Triumph Through Christ, nd. Talks given at the Upwey Convention, 1942-43.

United Church Action, What is it?, nd.

Abolishing God, nd. A reply to Professor Anderson of Sydney University.

Revelation and Inspiration, nd. Theological Students Fellowship lecture, [1949].

Memories Crowd Upon Me, London, 1949. Autobiographical.

Priesthood, Ministry and Apostolic Succession, nd.

Is this Anglicanism?, nd.

The Problem of Sex in relation to Natural and Social Developments, nd. [c.1950]. Published by the Australian Society for the Eradication of Venereal Disease.

The Proposed Roman Catholic University, nd.

Loved and Hated, the Problem of Martin Luther, Sydney, nd. [1950s?].

Marriage and Education, nd. A reply to Dr. Rumble.

The Case for Protestantism, Sydney, nd. [1950s?] Over twenty of Hammond's broadcast talks.

What is an Evangelical?, Sydney, 1956.

Must I Confess?, Sydney, 1959. Aimed at Anglo-Catholic practice.

From Slave to Saint, Sydney, nd. [1950s?]. On Patrick.

The following were written anonymously:

Simple Investigations of Great Truths, Dublin, nd. [1920s?].

Did Protestants Deliberately Mistranslate the Scriptures?, Sydney, nd.

C. CONTRIBUTOR

'Consciousness and the Sub-Conscious', an appendix to E. Digges La Touche, *The Person of Christ in Modern Thought*, London, 1912.

Debate in *The Church of Christ*, London, 1923.

'The Church of England' in the AEGM Series, London, 1923.

'The Fiat of Authority' in R. Howden, ed., *Evangelicalism*, London, 1925.

'Prayers and Masses for the Dead' and 'Priestcraft and Ireland' in *Protestantism*, the Report of the United

Protestant Congress, London, October 1922. London, 1923.

'The Schoolmen of the Later Middle Ages' in A. J. McDonald, *The Evangelical Doctrine of the Holy Communion*, London, nd. [1928].

'The Significance of the Death of Christ' in F.D. Coggan, *From the Manger to the Throne*, London, 1932.

'Post-Reformation Theology in the Church of Ireland' in W. Bell and N. D. Emerson, eds., *The Church in Ireland, 432-1932*, Dublin, 1932.

'Bible Study Circles' in *Effective Witness in Strategic Centres*, London, 1933.

Contributor to J. Harred, *The Church and the 20th Century*, London, 1936.

Preface to *The Bathurst Ritual Case*, Sydney, 1948.

Foreword to A. E. Hughes, *Lift Up A Standard*, London, 1948.

Contributor to J. S. Hart, *A Commentary on the Draft Constitution of the Church of England in Australia*, Sydney, nd. [1950s?].

Preface to W. Hogben, *Spiritual Dynamite*, Sydney, 1956.

'Malines Conversation', 'Catholic Emancipation', 'Maynooth', 'Moral Theology', 'Unam Sanctam', in *The Protestant Dictionary*, 1933.

Hammond also contributed in committee to:

Roman Claims, Dublin, 1931. A Church of Ireland catechism on the Roman controversy.

Evangelical Belief, London, 1935. The Inter-Varsity Fellowship's explanation of its doctrinal basis.

D. MAGAZINES AND JOURNALS TO WHICH
    HAMMOND REGULARLY CONTRIBUTED

The Catholic
The Church of Ireland Gazette
The Australian Church Record (many unsigned pieces)
Societas (the magazine of Moore College)
Glad Tidings (Journal of the Bible Union of Australia)
Evangelical Action (earlier entitled *Glad Tidings*)

E. EXTANT TYPESCRIPTS

Was the Reformation a Mistake? Held in the Irish Bible School Library.
Cranmer on the Lord's Supper. Held in Moore College Library. This is possibly a draft for a book Hammond intended to write.
Broadcast Talks. In the possession of the Rev B. Judd.
Lighter Moments in a Long Life. Held in Moore College and also in the Irish Bible School. A humorous autobiographical account of his youth and Dublin days.

F. MISCELLANEOUS AND FRAGMENTARY
    MANUSCRIPTS HELD IN:

Moore College, Sydney
Irish Church Missions, Dublin
Irish Bible School, Coalbrook, Thurles, Co. Tipperary
Reformed Theological College, Geelong
Representative Church Body Library, Dublin.
Christian Foundations. Held in Moore College. An earlier draft of *The New Creation*.

Appendix II

The Wit & Wisdom of T. C. Hammond

The following short quotes and epigrams from the writings of Hammond and from his attributed comments are offered as a sample of his sharpness and humour. No attempt has been made to divide wit from wisdom since, after all, the old usage of the word 'wit' shows how close to wisdom all true wit is.

It is much too great a simplification of human experience to declare outright that 'the bad' is identical with 'the uneconomic'. *Perfect Freedom,* p. 30.

Hasty generalisations are the bane of knowledge. Ibid., p. 97.

No doubt the pedant will be scandalised. Perhaps it will do him good. *Failed Light,* Preface.

It takes a long time to waken an Englishman. I am not English myself, being Irish I wake before I go to sleep. Ibid., p. 40.

They have in their minds this kind of notion, that a scientist is a pure searcher after truth, whereas a clergyman is a searcher after £.s.d. I hope the scientist gets further in his quest than the clergyman. Ibid., p. 53.

We can afford to be patient with these young people, and wait till they effervesce. Ibid., p. 122.

What exactly do you mean? Are you merely repeating German platitudes, or are you really thinking for yourselves? Ibid., p. 124.

I suppose dentists will be pulling teeth in the world to come Ibid., p. 81. (About a theology that robs God of judgment and presents heaven as a continuation of this world.)

When I read the daily newspapers I always keep a salt-cellar beside me. Ibid., p. 84.

Actually, someone sits in an office chair and writes these things. Ibid., p. 84. (On the 'infallibility' of leading articles in newspapers.)

The natural instinct to run off after familiar phrases must be steadily resisted. *Effective Witness*, p. 37. (On Bible study.)

The grass waves green before the eye of the ploughboy and the savant. With all the latter knows of its inner properties it is still green grass. *Evangelicalism*, p. 176.

Intolerance refuses to attach itself to any party. It is rampant amongst the people who are parading their liberalism. *Failed Light*, p. 109.

People say they can worship God in the open air. 'Yes' I reply, 'but do you ? You can't worship with a tennis racket or fish hooks.' Ibid., p. 117.

It would be a mercy for Christendom if the phraseology of many enthusiasts could be purged of inaccuracy, so that the glory of the Atoning Sacrifice would not be prejudiced in the minds of many earnest seekers. *In Understanding Be Men, p. 148.*

We need to remember that Christian Doctrine . . . is of value . . . in energising the spiritual life of the individual. Ibid., p. 13.

Error always takes its revenge. Ibid., p. 14.

Theology has its fashions and even its fads. Ibid.

Has it ever occurred to the reader that the Gnostics and semi-Pelagians abound in and around his college? Ibid., p. 22. (On the value of studying Church history.)

Safety lies in close definition. *Reasoning Faith*, p. 110.

But it must be pointed out that the human mind refuses to close its investigations with an unknown. Ibid., p. 29. (On agnosticism.)

It has often been pointed out that monkeys would warm themselves at a traveller's fire, but they have never been known to keep it alight by throwing fresh fuel on it. Ibid., p. 41. (On the unique human capacity for reflection.)

Agnosticism has gradually descended to Pessimism. Ibid., p. 44.

While it is quite true that we can become so precise as to be unreal, we can also become unreal through failing to be precise. *The New Creation*, p. 29.

The devil has no happy old people. In an address at Swanwick 1947. (Attributed to Hammond by Herbert Carson.)

It will be a great day for Christianity when its devotees

rediscover the actual grandeur of the Person they dimly worship. *In Understanding Be Men*, p. 132.

We train men not mice. *Societas*, Michelmas Term, 1944. (On Moore College students' War record.)

I believe in a simple Gospel but not a silly Gospel. *Pivotal Points*.

Troops should be entertained, Yes, but not at the expense of dishonour to Almighty God. *Sunday Amusements*.

Consecration is more than chorus singing, more than prayer meetings, more than conventions. Consecration is in its fullest sense the surrendering of every energy God has given us to the control of the Holy Spirit to the fulfilment of His will. *Pivotal Points*.

Orators are as common as gooseberries where I come from. *Good News for Bad Men*.

Do not shut your eyes and ears and then open your mouth. *Pivotal Points*. (On discipline.)

If a young man has anything to offer he'll be a bit troublesome. (Attributed.)

The trouble is some people don't know the difference between the beautiful and the sublime. (Attributed: after an argument about flowers in church.)

The 17th article (*i.e.* of the 39 Articles) needs to be explained, but not explained away! Quoted by N.D. Emerson in an obituary. (The comment is on the doctrine of predestination.)

SIGN NO DOCUMENTS. *Marriage, My Choice*. (On Protestant-Roman Catholic marriages. Capitals in original.)

If you are in a Church remain in it until you are satisfied from a study of the Word of God that you are being asked to accept teaching which is not only [not] contained in the Scriptures but is in manifest contradiction to the truth therein revealed. But do not act hastily. God in His providence placed you where you are and nothing but true conviction can justify you in leaving the religious body to which you have been attached. This applies equally to Roman Catholics and Protestants. *Evangelical Action*, Sept. 1957.

I believe that segregation is the forerunner of suspicion and hostility. From a tape recording. (On segregated schools.)

We do not grasp God. He lays hold of us. 'But that' says the unthinking 'lands you in Calvinism'. Wherever it lands us, if it brings us to God, to Him be the glory. *The New Creation*, p. 111.

Appendix III

Select Bibliography

Acheson, A. R., 'The Evangelicals in the Church of Ireland 1784-1854' (unpublished Ph.D. thesis, Queen's University of Belfast, 1967).

d'Alton, I., *Protestant Society and Politics in Cork, 1812-1844* (Cork, 1980).

Finnegan, M. A., *A History of the Irish Church* (forthcoming).

Hughes, A.. E., *Lift Up a Standard* (London, 1948).

Judd, S. & Cable, K., *Sydney Anglicans* (Sydney, 1987).

Loane, M. L., *A Centenary History of Moore College, Sydney* (Sydney, 1955).

Loane, M. L., *Mark These Men* (Canberra, 1985).

Philips, W. A. ed., *History of the Church of Ireland*, Vol. III (1933).

White, J., *Minority Report* (London, 1975).

Wilson, David A., *A New Breed of Irishmen* (Dublin, 1985).

Notes

Preface

1. An expression Hammond himself uses in *Age-Long Questions*, p. vii, with reference to Bishop Butler, the opponent of Deism.
2. *Perfect Freedom*, p. 284.

Chapter 1   Land of Saints and Sinners?

1. *Protestantism in answer to Romanism, Anglo-Catholicism and Modernism* (Report of United Protestant Congress 1922), p. 102.
2. H. Seddall, *Edward Nangle* (London, 1884), p. xxiv.
3. A. Dallas, *The Story of the Irish Church Missions* (London, 1867), p. 2.

Chapter 2   Evangelism in Victorian Ireland

1. W. A. Phillips, *History of the Church of Ireland,* vol. III, p. 344.
2. Mrs Madden, *Memoir of Rt. Rev. Robert Daly* (London, 1975), p. 292.
3. See D. Bowen, *Souperism, Myth or Reality* (Cork, 1970).
4. Tape Recording of T. C. Hammond (Irish Bible School).
5. A. R. Acheson, *The Evangelicals in the Church of Ireland, 1784-1854* (Unpublished thesis, Queen's University, Belfast).

Chapter 3   The Boy Preacher

1. Original document in the possession of the Hammond family.
2. *Light and Life*, p. 3.
3. From a biographical interview given by Hammond, *Societas*, 1953. Hammond's memory seems to have failed him here. This event could not have happened in Cork, as the dates do not coincide with any Royal visit. Perhaps it happened in England while he was visiting relatives.
4. Typescript *Lighter Moments in a Long Life*, p. 1.
5. Minute books, Cork YMCA.
6. Ibid.
7. *Bright Words* (Faith Mission Magazine), April 1956.
8. *Perfect Freedom*, p. 274. Note also the careful way he distinguishes conversion and regeneration in *In Understanding Be Men*, p.178 and the very full discussion of the matter in *The New Creation*, pp. 28f.
9. S. Watson, *From Darkness to Light*, The life and work of Mrs Baeyertz, nd.
10. R. Hobson, *What Hath God Wrought* (London, 1907).
11. T. C. Hammond, *Memories Crowd Upon Me*.
12. Tape Recording, T. C. Hammond.
13. Typescript, *Lighter Moments in a Long Life*, p. 4.
14. Recollection of Mrs Allshire, niece.
15. Tape Recording, T. C. Hammond.
16. Records, Christian Brothers, Kells, Co. Meath.
17. ICM Trainees Record Book.
18. Incidents from *Memories Crowd Upon Me* and *Lighter Moments in a Long Life*, and Tape Recording, T. C. Hammond.

Chapter 4   A Parish in Dublin

1. N. Hubbard, *Almost a Martyr's Fire* (Sydney, 1984).
2. Author of Commentaries on Exodus, Mark and Galatians

in the Tyndale Commentaries series published by Inter-Varsity Press.

3. Anecdote related in interview with Archbishop G. O. Simms.
4. Minute book of St. Kevin's Parish (Representative Church Body Library, Dublin).
5. Ibid.
6. Tape recording of T. C. Hammond.
7. *Daily Express* (Dublin), August 29, 1912.
8. Minute book of St. Kevin's.
9. *Daily Express* (Dublin), October 13, 1912.
10. Family recollections, kindly given by his daughter Doris Taplin.
11. Minute book, St. Kevin's.

Chapter 5   At The Irish Church Missions

1. *Protestantism in Answer to Romanism, Anglo-Catholicism and Modernism,* pp. 101f.
2. Recollection of former Mission worker (ICM).
3. *Lighter Moments in a Long Life.* We can surmise from his writings that his answer to this question involved showing that the majority of the Fathers of the church of the early centuries did not equate Peter with the Rock.
4. Recollection of a former Mission worker (ICM).
5. Recalled by a former Mission worker.
6. Recollection of William Scarlett, author's uncle.
7. J. J. Long, *Medical Missions in Ireland* (Dublin, 1925).
8. Tape Recording, T. C. Hammond.
9. *Church of Ireland Gazette,* December 4, 1925.
10. Recollections of Horan Family.
11. Tape Recording, T. C. Hammond.
12. Letter to the author from the late Douglas Johnson.
13. *The New Creation,* p. 5.
14. All quotes to the end of the chapter are from *Banner of Truth in Ireland,* April/June, 1936.

Chapter 6   'To Australia's Sunny Shore . . .'

1. For the following section see Judd and Cable, *Sydney Anglicans*.
2. M.L. Loane, *History of Moore College*.
3. Recollection of former student.
4. I. Shevill, *Half Time* (Brisbane, 1966), p. 10.
5. The remainder of this chapter is largely based on recollections of former students.
6. Letter to author. See also Foreword.

Chapter 7   Australia at Large

1. *The Bathurst Ritual Case* (Sydney nd. [1949]).
2. Recollections of former students.
3. Anecdote by Hammond's daughter.
4. The term *rite* has reference to actions done in a ritual fashion, particularly with reference to the sacrament of baptism, while *recte* refers to actions performed in the right way.
5. Anecdote by Hammond's daughter.
6. Family recollections.
7. One such occasion, three months before he died, being the only time the present writer met him.
8. *In Understanding Be Men*, p. 240.
9. A. Berkley, *Vox Reformata* (November 1979).

Chapter 8   Books and Theology

1. See page 88 for circumstances.
2. See page 61 for circumstances.
3. Broadcast talk, Judd papers.
4. *In Understanding Be Men*, p. 204.
5. *A Century of Service* (Dublin YMCA, 1940), p. 98.